Understanding

The Adventures of Huckleberry Finn

New and future titles in the Understanding Great Literature series include:

Understanding

The Adventures of Huckleberry Finn

UNDERSTANDING GREAT LITERATURE

Gary Wiener

Lucent Books
P.O. Box 289011
San Diego, CA 92198-9011

Library of Congress Cataloging-in-Publication Data

Wiener, Gary.
Understanding The Adentures of Huckleberry Finn / by
Gary Wiener.
    p. cm. — (Understanding great literature)
Includes bibliographical references (p.) and index.
    Summary: Covers the biography of Samuel Langhorne
Clemens, historical background, the plot and characters of
Huckleberry Finn, and includes a literary analysis of the book.
ISBN 1-56006-785-3 (lib. : alk. paper)
    1. Twain, Mark, 1835–1910. Adventures of Huckleberry
Finn—Juvenile literature. 2. Adventure stories, American—
History and criticism—Juvenile literature. 3. Finn, Huckleberry
(Fictitious character)—Juvenile literature. 4. Boys in literature—
Juvenile literature. [1. Twain, Mark, 1835–1910. Adventures of
Huckleberry Finn. 2. American literature—History and criticism.]
I. Title. II. Series.
    PS1305 .W57 2001
    813'.4—dc21

00-012856

Contents

FOREWORD

"Except for a living man, there is nothing more wonderful than a book!" wrote the widely respected nineteenth-century teacher and writer Charles Kingsley. A book, he continued, "is a message to us from human souls we never saw. And yet these [books] arouse us, terrify us, teach us, comfort us, open our hearts to us as brothers." There are many different kinds of books, of course; and Kingsley was referring mainly to those containing literature—novels, plays, short stories, poems, and so on. In particular, he had in mind those works of literature that were and remain widely popular with readers of all ages and from many walks of life.

Such popularity might be based on one or several factors. On the one hand, a book might be read and studied by people in generation after generation because it is a literary classic, with characters and themes of universal relevance and appeal. Homer's epic poems, the *Iliad* and the *Odyssey*, Chaucer's *Canterbury Tales*, Shakespeare's *Hamlet* and *Romeo and Juliet*, and Dickens's *A Christmas Carol* fall into this category. Some popular books, on the other hand, are more controversial. Mark Twain's *Huckleberry Finn* and J. D. Salinger's *The Catcher in the Rye*, for instance, have their legions of devoted fans who see them as great literature; while others view them as less than worthy because of their racial depictions, profanity, or other factors.

Still another category of popular literature includes realistic modern fiction, including novels such as Robert Cormier's *I Am the Cheese* and S. E. Hinton's *The Outsiders*. Their keen social insights and sharp character portrayals have consistently reached out to and captured the imaginations of many teenagers and young adults; and for this reason they are often assigned and studied in schools.

These and other similar works have become the "old standards" of the literary scene. They are the ones that people most often read, discuss, and study; and each has, by virtue of its content, critical success, or just plain longevity, earned the right to be the subject of a book examining its content. (Some, of course, like the *Iliad* and *Hamlet*, have been the subjects of numerous books already; but their literary stature is so lofty that there can never be too many books about them!) For millions of readers and students in one generation after another, each of these works becomes, in a sense, an adventure in appreciation, enjoyment, and learning.

The main purpose of Lucent's Understanding Great Literature series is to aid the reader in that ongoing literary adventure. Each volume in the series focuses on a single literary work that a majority of critics and teachers view as a classic and/or that is widely studied and discussed in schools. A typical volume first tells why the work in question is important. Then follow detailed overviews of the author's life, the work's historical background, its plot, its characters, and its themes. Numerous quotes from the work, as well as by critics and other experts, are interspersed throughout and carefully documented with footnotes for those who wish to pursue further research. Also included is a list of ideas for essays and other student projects relating to the work, an appendix of literary criticisms and analyses by noted scholars, and a comprehensive annotated bibliography.

The great nineteenth-century American poet Henry David Thoreau once quipped: "Read the best books first, or you may not have a chance to read them at all." For those who are reading or about to read the "best books" in the literary canon, the comprehensive, thorough, and thoughtful volumes of the Understanding Great Literature series are indispensable guides and sources of enrichment.

What a Trouble It Was

There is a short list of great American novels that includes Hawthorne's *The Scarlet Letter*, Melville's *Moby Dick*, Fitzgerald's *The Great Gatsby*, and Twain's *The Adventures of Huckleberry Finn*. But when one talks about *the* great American novel, *Huckleberry Finn* is the likely choice. Ironically, it is not the most well crafted or intellectually profound or aesthetically perfect of the group. In fact, the beginning is pretty much a boy's book, the middle is episodic and not entirely coherent, and the ending—well, many critics think the ending is just plain bad. And yet, as Ernest Hemingway observes in *The Green Hills of Africa*, *The Adventures of Huckleberry Finn* occupies a central place in the history of American letters. "All modern American literature," Hemingway's persona intones, "comes from one book by Mark Twain called *Huckleberry Finn*. . . . There was nothing before. There has been nothing as good since."[1]

As ancient Greece had *The Iliad* and *The Odyssey*; Rome, *The Aeneid*; France, *The Song of Roland*; Spain, *El Cid*; and England, *Beowulf* and *Paradise Lost*, America has *The Adventures of*

Huckleberry Finn. The late critic Clifton Fadiman has called it "the nearest thing we have to a national epic."[2] It is a novel that speaks for all of America, depicting its people at their best and at their worst. It explores the social system from the lowest caste in early-nineteenth-century middle America, the slaves, to the highest, the aristocrats. The book even throws in a king and a duke, however dubiously, for good measure. Its hero, Huckleberry Finn, is not a great warrior who battles valiantly and saves a nation. And yet he is. Huck Finn, the rogue hero of the novel, is a thirteen-year-old boy, but his battle with the system that enslaves men unjustly is as noble and Herculean a struggle as any the heroes of old encountered. To save his friend and companion, Huck, armed only with his wits, must fly in the face of an entire nation, an entire social code. No epic hero ever had greater odds stacked against him.

A Troublesome Book to Write

"If I'd a knowed what a trouble it was to make a book I wouldn't a tackled it and ain't agoing to no more,"[3] Huck says on the very last page of *The Adventures of Huckleberry Finn*. Huck could be speaking for Twain, who had an exceedingly difficult time writing the book. He began with the intention of writing a "boy's book," a sequel, of sorts, to *Tom Sawyer*. But the Twain who wrote *Huckleberry Finn* was older and wiser and more jaded than the author who wrote its predecessor. After the early hijinks of Tom and Huck, the book turns toward more serious issues, in particular, that of one man's owning another. Twain sets Huck and the slave Jim on a quest for freedom. But once he got to the point where Huck and Jim's raft sails past Cairo, Illinois, and the potential sanctuary offered by the Ohio River, the writing of the book stalled. The question Huck would later pose to the king and duke, "Goodness sakes, would a runaway [slave] run *south?*"[4] left Twain without an answer. Having composed approximately four hundred manuscript pages, Twain left off writing in 1876. He tried again in the autumn of 1879 but wrote only a few chapters until the summer of 1883, when he resumed in earnest. For Twain as well as Huck, it was trouble to make a book.

A Troublesome Book to Read

The problems were just beginning. *The Adventures of Huckleberry Finn* has come under continual attack from the early days of its publication, and while the motivation for such attacks has

Mark Twain's unflinching look at slavery in The Adventures of Huckleberry Finn *has incited controversy for over one hundred years.*

changed over the years, the book is still under indictment, and seemingly always will be. As the title of a film broadcast on the Public Broadcasting System (PBS) in 2000 suggests, *Huckleberry Finn* was a book "Born to Trouble." While there were many positive early reviews of *Huckleberry Finn* after its publication in 1884, the early attacks on the novel are most remembered. In Massachusetts the Concord Public Library banned the book in 1885. Denver, Colorado, followed in 1902, and the Brooklyn Public Library removed it from the children's room because "Huck not only itched but he scratched, and . . . he said sweat when he should have said perspiration."[5]

Huckleberry Finn weathered such attacks and settled into a position as one of the most read books in American schools until a new challenge emerged. In the last half of the twentieth century, African Americans began, with increasing regularity, to decry the book's alleged racism. Two objections were prominent: the depiction of Jim was said to be a racial stereotype, and the use of the vulgar term "nigger" was similarly offensive to African American readers.

An Enduring Message

For all of these objections and more, *Huckleberry Finn* has endured. The novel confronts, head-on, the greatest shame of early American society, and writing about controversial subjects inevitably causes more controversy. Perhaps, as with many great books, it is the subtlety of Twain's method and message that has caused so much conflict. Twain never says, "Slavery is evil." His theme must emerge through the complex internal debate of a barely educated boy who has been brainwashed by "sivilization" about the merits of the slave system, yet who still understands, deep in his heart, that something is gravely wrong with a system that makes one man another's possession. A careful and open-minded reading of *The Adventures of Huckleberry Finn* will enable the reader to see the treasure that lies within the so-called "trash."

CHAPTER ONE

Biography of Samuel Langhorne Clemens

S amuel Langhorne Clemens's father and mother, John Marshall and Jane Lampton Clemens, were both born of poor but gentrified parents. Their families had been slaveholders and landowners in Virginia, and both could claim some slim ancestral link to power in England, the home of their forebears. John could trace his line to one of the judges whose decision doomed King Charles I of England to beheading in 1649, while Jane's ancestors were the earls of Durham, England. Twain's lifelong preoccupation with royalty stemmed in part from this connection, and he even whimsically imagined himself as the earl of Durham. His fascination with claims to noble titles manifested itself in many ways, including in the satirical portraits of the king and duke in *The Adventures of Huckleberry Finn*.

Jane Lampton and John Clemens had met in Kentucky. After their marriage, the impoverished couple remained in Jane's hometown of Columbia, Kentucky, for a few years until the hope of better prospects led them to Gainesboro, Tennessee, where their first child, Orion, was born in July 1825. Not long after, they moved again, to Jamestown, Tennessee, where John opened a store, practiced law, and bought up thousands of acres of land, which turned out to be nearly worthless. The Clemenses had more children: Pamela in 1827; Pleasant Hannibal, who died in infancy, in 1828; and Margaret in 1830. In 1831 the family moved again, just nine miles north to Pall Mall, Tennessee, where Benjamin, their fifth child, was born in June 1832.

But their prospects were no better in Pall Mall. In 1834 the family moved west to the tiny town of Florida, Missouri, where Jane's sister, Martha Ann, lived with her husband, John Quarles, a successful, respected, and popular farmer. John and Jane Clemens and their four children settled into a two-room frame house, and on November 30, 1835, two months premature, Mark Twain was born Samuel Langhorne Clemens. The night Sam was born, Halley's comet appeared in the sky. It would not be visible again until he died in April 1910.

John Clemens attempted shopkeeping in Florida and became a justice of the peace in the county court, thus attaining the title of judge. He would serve as the model for Judge Thatcher in *Tom Sawyer* and *Huckleberry Finn*. The people in Twain's life often found their way into his fiction. In 1895 Twain told interviewer Luke Pease, "I don't believe an author . . . ever lived, who created a character. It was always drawn from his recollection of someone he had known."[6]

Little Sam in Hannibal

"Little Sam," as Twain was known, was a sickly child, surviving against all odds the trials brought on by his premature birth and numerous bouts with disease. Growing up was no given in frontier Missouri. Sam's elder sister, Margaret, would die at the age of nine and Benjamin at age ten.

In 1838 Henry, the last Clemens child, was born. The next year the family moved to Hannibal, Missouri, the town that would forever become associated with Mark Twain. As

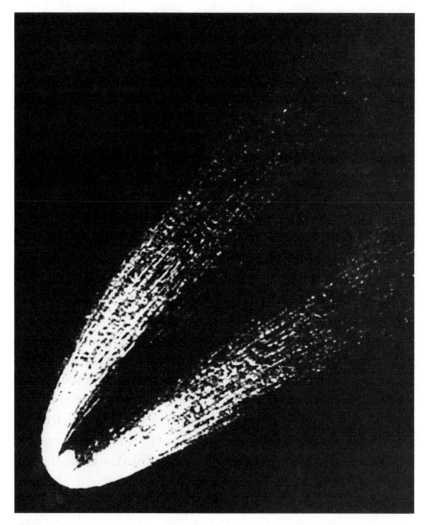

Halley's comet appeared on Mark Twain's birth date in 1835. In a peculiar coincidence, it was not seen again until his death in 1910.

biographer Andrew Hoffman writes, "Hannibal presented Sam with frightening and entrancing adventures. Though he had been transplanted from a familiar town . . . the great Mississippi River flowed just a hundred yards from [his] door."[7]

Especially exciting to Sam, and every other boy in Hannibal, were the great steamboats that chugged along the river. The riverboat captains and pilots were great heroes, larger-than-life figures whom every boy wished to emulate. This youthful fascination with steamboats is illustrated in *Tom Sawyer*, when Ben Rogers comes walking down the street, he is "giving a long, melodious whoop, at intervals, followed by a deep-toned ding-dong-dong, ding-dong-dong, for he was personating a steamboat."[8]

Five-year-old Samuel Clemens was sent to a private school where the teaching included religious instruction. On one occasion the teacher informed the attentive Sam that he could receive whatever he wished through prayer. Young Sam prayed for gingerbread, and soon after the opportunity presented itself for him to steal a slab from a classmate who was looking the other way. Twain writes, "I never enjoyed an answer to a prayer more than I enjoyed that one; and I was a convert, too."[9]

Far more exciting than Sam's schooling were his yearly two- to-three-month visits to the farm of his uncle John A. Quarles. Sam stayed on the Florida, Missouri, farm with his uncle and aunt and their eight children every year from the time he was four until he was eleven or twelve. Sam passed the summers playing and, in the process, befriended many slaves. According to Twain, the Quarles farm was the model for the Phelps plantation in *Huckleberry Finn*.

As the Clemenses' fortunes fell, they were forced to lower their lifestyle, ultimately losing homes, land, furniture, and even their slave girl. Orion was apprenticed to a printer in St. Louis. By 1846 the Clemenses could only make ends meet by sharing a home with another family. There was always the hope that someday the land John Clemens owned in Tennessee would make the family rich. But such a scenario never came to pass.

In March 1847 John Clemens, having weakened himself greatly by putting all of his energies into running for the office of clerk of the surrogate court, fell sick with pneumonia and died. This disaster occurred, Twain would write, "just at the very moment when our fortunes had changed and we were about to be comfortable once more."[10] Sam was overcome with guilt at his father's death, convinced that he could have been a better son, one who did not defy his father's commands so often.

A Printer's Fortunes

Sam attended school until 1848 then became a full-time printer's apprentice under Joseph Ament, owner of the *Hannibal Courier*. He drew no salary but nevertheless worked hard at his new trade, learning to set type and, when the need arose, serving as a reporter or editor.

In 1850 Sam's oldest brother, Orion, returned to Hannibal and bought a weekly newspaper, the *Western Union*. Sam left Ament to work for his brother, who promised him $3.50 a week, a salary that Sam was never able to collect, for Orion was as poor a businessman as his father before him.

Sam soon began to publish his own articles. On January 16, 1851, "A Gallant Fireman," his first published work, appeared in the *Western Union*. Other articles soon followed and found a national audience. "The Dandy Frightening the Squatter" appeared in the Boston paper, the *Carpet-Bag*, on May 1, 1852. A week later Sam published "Hannibal, Missouri" in the Philadelphia *American Courier*.

In June 1853 Sam set off on his own, leaving Hannibal behind. As biographer Dixon Wechter suggests, for the remainder of his career, his "genius always swung like a compass toward his fourteen years' childhood and adolescence in Hannibal," for "no major artist ever made more of his boyhood than did Samuel Clemens."[11]

Sam made stops in St. Louis, New York City, and Philadelphia. In each city he found work as a printer but earned little money. By early 1854 he grew homesick and took the train back to St. Louis, where he found work at the *Evening News*.

A year later he moved to Keokuk, Iowa, and was reunited with Orion, who had recently married. Orion persuaded Sam to work on his new venture, a print shop, for the lofty sum of $5 a week. But, as before, Orion proved to be a poor businessman and Sam was rarely paid.

After reading about an exploration of the Amazon River, Sam decided he would make his fortune in South America. One day he found a $50 bill on the street. When no one claimed it, Sam had seed money to begin his journey. He stopped in Cincinnati, where he worked in a printing office to earn more money for his trip. At his boardinghouse Sam met a Scotsman named Macfarlane. The two men engaged in long discussions on topics such as politics and religion. Biographer Andrew Hoffman summarizes Macfarlane's influence on the man who would become Mark Twain:

> [Macfarlane] outlined his pre-Darwinian theory of evolution, maintaining that man's consciousness was a developmental dead end, a fact that bumped humans from the top of the evolutionary ladder to the bottom. Sympathetic to the blamelessness of nonconscious animals, Sam began to regard the human race with deep ambivalence. He questioned whether the capacity for thought, which distinguished humans from lower animals, actually did raise the moral value of human beings.[12]

The Mississippi and Points West

In April 1857 Sam continued his trip down the Mississippi, still planning to continue on to South America. He booked passage on the *Paul Jones*, a steamboat piloted by Horace Bixby. The two struck up a friendship, and Sam persuaded Bixby to teach him how to be a riverboat pilot. Forgetting about his trip to South America, he began the difficult task of learning every idiosyncrasy of the great river from St. Louis to

New Orleans. On April 9, 1859, following a two-year apprenticeship, Sam received his pilot's license.

A steamboat pilot commanded great prestige as well as a large salary. Sam might have continued in this lucrative career for the rest of his working life, but in 1861 the Civil War began. He returned to Hannibal, where sentiment ran toward the Confederacy. Several of his friends had joined a volunteer militia, and Sam, embracing their zealotry, followed suit. But he served for only two weeks and never saw serious action. He would deliberately avoid the remainder of the four-year conflict.

In 1861 Orion was appointed secretary to the governor of the Nevada Territory. Sam used money he had earned as a pilot to pay both their fares out there. After a trip later recounted in Twain's *Roughing It*, the pair reached Carson City, Nevada, on August 14, 1861. Carson City was a boomtown. Nevada mines were giving forth tons upon tons of silver, and there were great fortunes to be made. Even Sam tried his hand at mining but found the work too physically demanding.

Readers back east were hungry for tales of the "Wild West," and some of Sam's letters back home were published in the Keokuk, Iowa, paper. He also submitted humorous letters to Nevada's leading newspaper, the Virginia City *Territorial Enterprise*. In the summer of 1862, he was offered a $25-a-week job with the *Enterprise*.

Mark Twain: Reporter and Yarn Spinner

Virginia City, located twelve miles northwest of Carson City, sat atop the famous Comstock Lode, the richest silver discovery ever made in the United States. As the *Enterprise*'s lone reporter, Twain scoured the streets for interesting stories. He became well known for his tall tales and comic writings, as well as for the clever hoaxes, popular at the time, that he would perpetrate on his readers. Several months after his arrival, Sam told his editor that he wished to sign his articles with a new name, "Mark Twain." The pseudonym was a holdover from his days as a riverboat pilot. "Mark Twain" meant that the water was two fathoms deep and signified safe passage. The new moniker appeared in print for the first time in February 1863. In the words of biographer John Lauber,

The youthful Twain first worked as a reporter at the Territorial Enterprise, *once Nevada's leading newspaper.*

[The pen name's] rightness seems to have been instantly recognized. He promptly became . . . "Mark Twain" . . . to the Western public and "Mark" to most of his Western friends. . . . He would continue to be "Sam" only to his mother, sister, and brother, and to a very few of his oldest friends. Two of the three closest friends of his later life, the writer William Dean Howells and the Standard Oil magnate H. H. Rogers, called him "Clemens"—a choice reflecting their own formality. . . . To the most intimate of them, Joe Twichell, his minister and Hartford neighbor, he would always be "Mark." To his wife, he would be "Youth" in private and "Mr. Clemens" in public. In business matters he was of course "Mr. Clemens"; to the reading public and the world at large he has always been "Mark Twain."[13]

The new Mark Twain's reputation skyrocketed. He was known throughout the territory, and his writings were reprinted in numerous newspapers.

On the Move

Ever nomadic, Twain was never comfortable in Virginia City. As he would recount in *Roughing It,* "I wanted to see San Francisco. I wanted to go somewhere. I wanted—I did not know *what* I wanted. I had the 'spring fever' and wanted a change, principally, no doubt."[14]

When the newspaper's editor took a trip and left Twain in charge, he used the freedom to bring on trouble. In one of a series of offenses, he insulted James Laird, the editor of a rival paper, the *Union,* and a duel was proposed. In Twain's autobiography, he spins a yarn about how his second, Steve Gillis, shot the head off a bird just as Laird was coming over a ridge to engage Twain. Laird thought it had been Twain's startlingly accurate shot and immediately called off the contest. But biographers have added this account to Twain's gallery of self-aggrandized memoirs. Twain's telling suggests that he left Nevada soon after to avoid being jailed for the crime of dueling, but modern biographers believe it is more likely he left to avoid such an encounter in the first place.

Twain arrived in San Francisco in June 1864. Now twenty-eight years old, he found work as the only reporter for the *Morning Call*. But he soon grew disenchanted with the paper, and conflicts with the editor led him to leave. Twain began writing for a new literary weekly, the *Californian*, penning sketches that brought him a mere $12 a month. In desperate financial shape, he considered taking a job as a government riverboat pilot, but a friend talked him out of it.

So Twain traveled to the Mother Lode hills of California, where he attempted to eke out a living as a pocket miner. It was here that Twain first heard a yarn about a man who entered his frog into a jumping contest. From the raw material of this popular tale, Twain weaved a polished story. On the advice of a friend, the famous comic writer Artemus Ward, he sent "Jim Smiley and His Jumping Frog" to the *New York Saturday Press*, where it was published. The story was an immediate hit and was reprinted around the country. It would eventually be re-titled "The Celebrated Jumping Frog of Calaveras County" and become an American classic.

Twain returned to San Francisco in February 1865. Money again became the critical need in his life. He found work as the San Francisco correspondent for the Virginia City *Territorial Enterprise*, but restlessness caught up with him, and in 1866 he was off to the Sandwich Islands, now Hawaii, as a special correspondent for the Sacramento *Daily Union*. During his four-month stay, he sent a series of humorous, clever, insightful pieces back to readers in the States, and his reputation grew. Back in San Francisco, seeking to benefit financially from his growing reputation, he tried the lecture circuit. Twain's presentation was a smash hit, and in the process he discovered a means of financial gain that he would fall back on for the remainder of his life.

According to biographer Bernard DeVoto, the seeds of everything that Twain would later pen could be found in the writings of his western adventure: "the humorist, the social satirist, the pessimist, the novelist of American character, Mark Twain exhilarated, sentimental, cynical, angry, and depressed, are all here. The rest is only development."[15]

With money gained from his lectures, Twain decided to journey back east, where a writer might make a greater reputation for himself than he could in the Wild West. Now thirty-one, he signed on as a travel correspondent with a major San Francisco paper, the *Alta California*, and after a long and arduous trip by ship and across Central America by boat and wagon, he arrived in New York in January 1867.

Twain wrote about New York for the *Alta California*. But he found the city dreary, and by March 1867 he was off to St. Louis, where he resumed lecturing. His return to Hannibal proved momentous, for it rekindled in him an interest in that town's affairs, and he wrote a burlesque history of Hannibal, including a tale of the town drunkard, Jimmy Finn, for the *Alta California*.

Marriage and Success

After his return to New York, Twain finally found a publisher for his first book, *The Celebrated Jumping Frog of Calaveras County, and Other Sketches*. In addition to the title story, the book consisted of about three dozen short pieces, many of which Twain had written for the *Californian*. Twain persuaded the *Alta California* to let him be a true travel correspondent. In June 1867 he booked passage on a pleasure cruise to the Mediterranean on the steamer *Quaker City*. Beyond giving the author the chance to see a part of the world about which he would later write (in *The Innocents Abroad*), the trip was notable for two people whose acquaintance Twain made.

The first was Mary Mason Fairbanks, wife of the publisher of the *Cleveland Herald*, who would become a lifelong friend. The second was a wealthy young man named Charley Langdon, whose father had sent him abroad to keep him out of trouble. In Charley's stateroom, Twain caught his first glimpse of Charley's sister, Olivia "Livy" Langdon, in an ivory miniature. Twain fell instantly in love with this beautiful daughter of an Elmira, New York, coal magnate. When he returned to the States, he began courting Livy Langdon. Their first date, Twain relates in his *Autobiography*, was to a reading by the English author Charles Dickens. "From that day . . . [she] has never been out of my mind nor heart,"[16] he asserted forty years later.

In July 1869 Twain published *The Innocents Abroad*. Twenty thousand copies were initially printed, but the book was a rousing success that necessitated additional printings. Almost seventy thousand copies sold in the first year. Twain's gentle satire of Old World pretensions was so endearing that the book was acclaimed even in Europe.

On February 2, 1870, Samuel Langhorne Clemens, the poor son of a ne'er-do-well midwestern lawyer, married into the wealthy Langdon clan. The couple's wedding present from Twain's new father-in-law, Jervis Langdon, was a large fully furnished house in Buffalo, New York. Twain had earlier purchased a share in the *Buffalo Express*, so the location of the home was quite appropriate.

The marriage of Twain and Livy Langdon was a happy one. Livy took some pains to civilize the rough-hewn Twain, who needed to tone down his penchant for swearing and to dress in a more gentlemanly fashion. She gently mocked his unquenchable fervor for life by calling him "Youth," but Twain doted on his wife absolutely. Unfortunately, their life together was attended by numerous tragedies. The first occurred when Jervis Langdon died of cancer in August 1870. Livy, who had spent months nursing him, suffered a nervous collapse upon his death. In November 1870 Livy gave birth prematurely to a son, Langdon Clemens, and for a time it seemed that neither mother nor child would survive.

Moving About Again

Feeling that the Buffalo house was no longer a happy place, Twain sold his stake in the *Buffalo Express* at a substantial loss, and the couple and their young child left that city to stay in Elmira, New York, with Livy's sister, at her family's hilltop home called Quarry Farm. There the couple found solace, and Twain began working steadily on a book about his western adventures that he would call *Roughing It*. In order to make up for his loss on the *Buffalo Express*, Twain also went back on the lecture circuit, which once again proved highly successful and lucrative.

With these proceeds, Sam and Livy moved to Hartford, Connecticut, where they rented a house. Early in 1872 *Roughing It* was published to critical acclaim. On March 19, 1872, Twain's second child, Olivia Susan Clemens, who would be known as Susy, was born. But less than two months later, the continually infirm little boy, Langdon Clemens, succumbed to illness and died. Guilt ridden, Twain blamed his own lapses in parenting for Langdon's death.

Again the couple sought to get away, spending the summer of 1872 on the Connecticut coast. In August Twain made a trip, alone, to London, to protect the copyrights on his books. His trip was highly successful. The English embraced the writer, greatly appreciating Twain's literary efforts and sense of humor.

Back in Hartford that winter, Twain settled into a life of enjoying his family and a host of new friends. One particularly fruitful relationship blossomed when Twain and the novelist Charles Dudley Warner bet their wives that together they could write a better novel than those which the women were reading.

The result was *The Gilded Age*, a novel whose title would provide a name for an entire period of American history.

Twain's success enabled the couple to plan a new home of their own in Hartford. In May 1873 Twain took Livy and Susy abroad, where they traveled through England and Scotland. Twain gave a series of lectures and was entertained by some of

Mark Twain is pictured here in 1870, the year of his marriage to Olivia Langdon. Although marked by tragedy, their union was strong and loving.

the greatest writers of the era, including the poet Robert Browning and Lewis Carroll, author of *Alice's Adventures in Wonderland.*

The Adventures of Huckleberry Finn

With the success of *The Gilded Age*, Twain's first book-length work after two travelogues, Twain felt confident that he could write other longer works of fiction. In Hartford Twain commissioned the building of a new home, "a nineteen-room architectural extravaganza that reflected both his originality and his status as a man of property."[17] As work on the house, one of the largest private dwellings in the city, proceeded, Twain began writing *The Adventures of Tom Sawyer*. The Cranes—his sister-in-law and her husband—had built him a writer's retreat on their property at Quarry Farm, and it was here, in April 1874, that Twain worked on *Tom Sawyer*. He set the book back in his hometown of Hannibal, Missouri, which he fictionalized as St. Petersburg. There were many interruptions, including the birth of his second daughter, Clara Langdon Clemens, on June 8, 1874, but the work went on steadily. Twain finished *Tom Sawyer* in July 1875. The book's publication was delayed until December 1876, and by this time Twain had already conceived of a sequel—*The Adventures of Huckleberry Finn*. After much deliberation as to whether *Tom Sawyer* would be aimed at adults or children, Twain, with the advice of his famous friend the novelist William Dean Howells, had settled on the latter. So, too, had he aimed at writing a "boy's book" when he began the sequel. "I like it only tolerably well, as far as I have got," he wrote William Dean Howells on August 9, 1876, "& may possibly pigeonhole or burn the MS [manuscript] when it is done."[18]

This book, too, saw many interruptions. In the summer of 1877, Twain began writing *The Prince and the Pauper*, a story of an English royal switch, while *Huck Finn* languished. This was not unusual. In 1906 Twain wrote, "There has never been a time . . . when my literary shipyard hadn't two or more half-finished ships on the ways, neglected and baking in the sun."[19] In April of the next year, in search of material for a new travel book his publisher had requested, Twain took his family abroad. They traveled in Germany and Switzerland, as well as in other European countries, while Twain worked on *A Tramp Abroad*. Back in the United States, Twain continued work on *The Prince and the Pauper*, recommenced writing *Huck Finn* briefly in 1879, and published *A Tramp Abroad* in March 1880. His last child, another daughter, Jane Lampton Clemens (who would be called Jean), was born at Quarry Farm in the summer of 1880.

Twain decided to publish an account of his Mississippi adventures, so in April 1882 he booked passage on the steamer *Gold Dust*. His trip, during which he was reacquainted with many of his old friends, not only resulted in *Life on the Mississippi*, but renewed the author's interest in his incomplete novel, *The Adventures of Huckleberry Finn*. He resumed work on the novel in the summer of 1883 at Quarry Farm and finished in late August. As critic Walter Blair says, "There is no evidence that he felt that the moment [of finishing *Huck Finn*] was an unusually important one. In retrospect, however, it is possible to see that it was a climax in Mark Twain's long career and also in American literary history."[20]

The novel was published first in England in 1884, and in the United States the next year. Readers expecting another *Tom Sawyer* were disappointed by the book's seriousness, and Huck's character raised the ire of those who felt he was an immoral thief and liar. But many also applauded Twain's attempt to deal with the serious theme of slavery, which had nearly torn the nation apart during the Civil War.

Financial Problems

In 1885 Twain set out once again on the lecture circuit, this time doing readings with the great southern writer George

Washington Cable, who had moved to Hartford. When Cable learned that Twain had never read Sir Thomas Malory's tales of King Arthur, he obtained a book for him, and Twain quickly took a great interest in the knights of the Round Table. The result of his fascination was the quirky novel *A Connecticut Yankee in King Arthur's Court*. Another of Twain's major projects at this time was to publish the memoirs of the great Civil War general Ulysses S. Grant. Grant, who was dying of cancer, nevertheless made a sustained effort to complete his life story, which Twain's own publishing company released shortly after his death in 1885. The book was a huge success, and Twain was able to send Grant's widow a royalty check for $200,000, an enormous amount of money at that time.

An 1836 painting by George Caitlin shows the broad sweep of the Mississippi River, a powerful force in Twain's life and work.

Twain was a brilliant author and a modestly successful inventor, but he had less of a mind for business. He invested hundreds of thousands of dollars over the years in failed inventions and often had to publish a new book or embark on the lecture circuit to make up for investment losses. The greatest example of Twain's failed investments came in the form of the Paige typesetter.

James W. Paige had invented a machine that would set type more quickly, accurately, and inexpensively than humans could do. But the Paige typesetter became a money pit for Mark Twain. A perfectionist, Paige kept tinkering with his machine for years while Twain poured more and more money—ultimately $190,000—into the machine. Twain's financial worries even affected his writing at times. Nevertheless, he continued to turn out new works, including *The Tragedy of Pudd'nhead Wilson* and *Tom Sawyer Abroad*. But his exorbitant expenditure on the Paige typesetter, along with the failure of his publishing company, led Twain to declare bankruptcy in 1894.

Pudd'nhead Wilson had been published and done well, and Twain continued work on his history of Joan of Arc, but he needed an additional source of income. He set off on a worldwide lecture tour, viewing lecturing as the best way to ease his financial crisis. Livy and two of his daughters accompanied him, but Susy, the eldest, who loathed sea voyages, stayed behind. The tour was a huge success. Twain lectured in the United States, Canada, Australia, New Zealand, India, Africa, and Europe, all the while sending large sums of money back to the States to pay off his creditors.

Back in Elmira, however, Susy Clemens had fallen sick and succumbed to meningitis. The family sailed home from Europe to attend her funeral. Twain was devastated at the loss of his twenty-four-year-old daughter. The family returned to Europe and dropped out of sight, mourning the loss of Susy privately in a rented London house. When, in 1896, many wondered if Twain the recluse were still alive, he made his famous pronouncement, "Just say the report of my death has been grossly exaggerated."[21]

Still, rumors persisted. As biographer Justin Kaplan notes, "In 1897 an American paper ran a headline five columns wide, 'Close of a Great Career,' and under it was the baseless story that Mark Twain, abandoned by his wife and daughters, was living in abject poverty."[22]

The family moved to Vienna, where Twain, disillusioned and depressed by all that had befallen him, began a series of satiric letters to Satan. Such was the tone of these letters that he never showed his work to Livy and directed that they be published after his death. *Letters from the Earth* did not appear until 1962. He also wrote *Following the Equator*, his last and darkest travel book, which recounts his world tour but also denounces European imperialism and all of the atrocities perpetrated by whites bringing "civilization" to Asia and Africa.

Tragedies Herald the End

Twain and his family finally returned to the United States, free of debt, in the fall of 1900. Twain had finally paid off all of his creditors in 1898. His return was a major media event, covered with great fanfare and generating public excitement. He moved to New York City, where he made appearances, lectured, and attended one party after another. In the words of Kaplan, "His favorite recreation . . . when he was not playing billiards, was to stroll up and down Fifth Avenue in his white suit, chat with the police, and be stared at."[23] He was writing less now, and the work he did produce was often darker and angrier and more political. One such piece was "The United States of Lyncherdom," a criticism of the treatment of African Americans in the South. The essay, however truthful, was so offensive that it was not published during his lifetime. Many of his critics felt that a "humorist" such as Twain should not delve into such matters at all.

The house built by Twain in Connecticut after Olivia's death. He spent his remaining years here and in Bermuda.

During these years Livy began to suffer from heart trouble. In August 1902 she endured a severe heart attack yet recovered; but a little over a year later, in Florence, Italy, she died from a second attack. Without his beloved wife, companion, editor, and conscience of thirty-three years, Twain would never be the same.

In 1906 Albert Bigelow Paine, a biographer, approached Twain with the concept of writing an authorized biography. Twain hired a stenographer, and the work commenced, with

Twain dictating an autobiographical mixture of fact, fiction, and whimsy. In 1907 Twain purchased land in Connecticut near where Paine lived and built a house. He would spend the rest of his life traveling mostly between Stormfield, as he named his new home, and Bermuda. In 1909 yet another tragedy befell the family. Twain's daughter Jean, who suffered from epilepsy, suffered a seizure in the bathtub and drowned. Twain had now lost his wife, a son, and two daughters. Only his daughter Clara, who had married the pianist Ossip Gabilowitsch a few months before, remained.

Twain himself had been suffering from a heart ailment for several years, and on April 21, 1910, with Halley's comet once again orbiting nearest the earth, he succumbed, bringing to a close the remarkable life of a man whom friend and fellow novelist William Dean Howells referred to as "the Lincoln of our literature."[24]

CHAPTER TWO

Historical Background

hile *The Adventures of Huckleberry Finn* was written in the nineteenth century and takes place in that same hundred-year period, there is a fifty-year difference between the time in which the novel is supposed to have taken place and the time of its composition. *The Adventures of Huckleberry Finn* is therefore, perhaps above all, a historical novel. The St. Petersburg that Twain depicts is the Hannibal, Missouri, of his remembrance, the Hannibal of the boy Sam Clemens, the author's real name for twenty-seven years before he adopted the pseudonym by which he would forever be known.

Romanticism and Realism

The difference between the post–Civil War America in which Twain wrote and the antebellum (or prewar) era that he depicted in the novel is at least as great as the difference between America before and after the Wright Brothers or World War II or the invention of the microchip.

Even the dominant literature of the pre– and post–Civil War eras was different. Romanticism, a mode of writing with which Twain has a good deal of fun in *The Adventures of Huckleberry Finn*, was a prevalent literary form before the war. Among the great masters of American romanticism were Edgar Allan Poe, Charles Brockden Brown, James Fenimore

Cooper, and Nathaniel Hawthorne. European romantics included poets such as Byron, Shelley, Keats, and Wordsworth, and the novelist Sir Walter Scott. Most romantic writers employed larger-than-life characters in their works, characters with great virtues and tragic faults that intensified the drama of the story line. English romantic novelists often favored kings and princesses and knights and noblemen in their adventures. But Mark Twain, along with many writers of fiction such as his friend William Dean Howells, preferred to write in a more realistic mode. Where many romantics favored exotic locales, bizarre occurrences, and larger-than-life heroes and heroines, realists grounded their fiction in the common everyday world. Huck, for example, is a barely literate, lower-class boy living in a small midwestern town. He is the kind of boy one could have run into in any town in any state in nineteenth-century America.

Twain continually disparages literary romanticism in *The Adventures of Huckleberry Finn*. It is no accident that the wrecked steamboat on the Mississippi that Huck and Jim board is called the *Walter Scott*. In the character of Tom Sawyer, Twain creates a boy who has been wholly taken in by romantic tales of adventure and is so engrossed in the world of make-believe that he sometimes ignores the real world. Thus, all of Tom's ridiculous schemes on the Phelps plantation are based on the words of "the best authorities," romance novelists whose works Tom has read and mistaken for literal truth. Books such as Alexandre Dumas's famous adventure novel, *The Count of Monte Cristo*, serve as Tom's blueprint for how to concoct a memorable dungeon experience and escape. Through all of the fun and hijinks, Twain's criticism of the nonsensical elements of the romance novel genre becomes apparent. One of Twain's famous essays, "Fenimore Cooper's Literary Offenses," mocks the absurdities in the novels of Cooper, a man often referred to as "the American [Sir Walter] Scott."

One serious fault Twain found with the romantic-era novel was in its use of dialogue. The conversation in a Fenimore Cooper novel, for example, seemed entirely false to Twain. Cooper's Native Americans spoke as if they had been educated in exclusive English schools rather than speaking in informal dialect. In "Fenimore Cooper's Literary Offenses," Twain writes of Cooper's dialogue, "When the personages of a tale deal in conversation, the talk [should] sound like human talk, and be talk such as human beings would be likely to talk in the given circumstances."[25] Richard Lederer succinctly puts Twain's revolutionary new way of capturing American dialogue in historical perspective:

> To see what Twain accomplished, compare the diction of his book with that of [American romantic novelist] Nathaniel Hawthorne's *The Scarlet Letter*, published only thirty-five years earlier. Listen . . . to little Pearl, the small daughter of Hester Prynne: "Nay, mother, I have told all I know. Ask yonder old man whom thou hast been talking with! It may be he can tell. But in good earnest now, mother dear, what does this scarlet letter mean?—and why dost thou wear it on thy bosom?" Does that sound like the language of a young American girl? Has any child anywhere ever talked like that?[26]

By contrast, in *The Adventures of Huckleberry Finn*, Twain strove to capture the speech of midwestern Americans exactly as he heard it. Readers can hear Huck's colloquial voice in the first line of the novel: "You don't know about me, without you have read a book by the name of '*The Adventures of Tom Sawyer*,' but that ain't no matter."[27]

Despite Twain's dissatisfaction with the romantic novel, *The Adventures of Huckleberry Finn* is indebted to literary romanticism. The scene in which Huck and Jim confront the robbers on the wrecked *Walter Scott* is straight out of romance novels, the idyllic natural setting on the raft is a romantic writer's dreamscape, and the numerous coincidences in the novel (such as Huck's stumbling onto the plantation of Tom's aunt and uncle) are hardly the stuff of strict realism.

The Reality of Slavery

Despite some borrowings from romances, the book's main plot, concerning the escaped slave Jim, is certainly a realistic one. Raised in an atmosphere that completely condoned slavery, Mark Twain had many of the same prejudices harbored by his peers. There were, according to Twain, "fifteen or twenty"[28] slaves on the farm of his uncle John Quarles, with whom he stayed each summer. Slavery in pre–Civil War Missouri was the natural order of things. Twain writes:

> In my schoolboy days I had no aversion to slavery. I was not aware that there was anything wrong about it. No one arraigned it in my hearing; the local papers said nothing against it; the local pulpit taught us that God approved it, that it was a holy thing and that the doubter need only look in the Bible if he wished to settle his mind—and then the texts were read aloud to us to make the matter sure; if the slaves themselves had an aversion to slavery they were wise and said nothing.[29]

Twain's father, John Clemens, had owned slaves "but by and by he sold them and hired others by the year from the farmers."[30] On the Quarles farm, young Sam befriended many slaves. With those his age, Twain writes, "we were in effect comrades." But, he adds, "I say in effect, using the phrase as a modification. We were comrades and yet not comrades; color and condition interposed a subtle line which both parties were conscious of and which rendered complete fusion impossible."[31]

Young Sam was particularly fond of one middle-aged slave, called Uncle Daniel, "a faithful and affectionate good friend, ally and adviser . . . whose sympathies were wide and warm and whose heart was honest and simple and knew no guile."[32] Uncle Daniel served Twain well in later years, for he is the model for Jim in *The Adventures of Huckleberry Finn*.

Twain's fondness for Uncle Daniel comes through clearly in Huck's friendship with Jim, and if his novel has any one single bias, it is antiracism. An objective reading of *The Adventures of Huckleberry Finn*, despite the racist attitude of its characters, bears this out. By setting the novel fifty years in the past, Twain was able to explore the ramifications of slavery as it was occurring, and he gave the pain and sadness and brutality of racism and slavery a face in Huck's friend and companion Jim.

A Model for Huckleberry Finn

In nineteenth-century Missouri, slaves were certainly at the bottom of the social order, but class distinctions among whites were also keenly felt. Though by birth the Clemenses belonged to the gentry, John Clemens's numerous schemes never panned out, and the family suffered a series of financial setbacks during Twain's youth that left them looking up with envy at the families of the town's professional men. Below the Clemenses were the poor whites, which in Hannibal included the town drunk, Jimmy Finn, and the Blankenship family. Young Tom Blankenship was the town pariah, and boys were warned never to play with him. Such warnings made his friendship all the more intriguing to young Sam, and Tom became the model for Huckleberry Finn.

As Twain writes in his autobiography:

> In *Huckleberry Finn* I have drawn Tom Blankenship exactly as he was. He was ignorant, unwashed, insufficiently fed; but he had as good a heart as ever any boy had. His liberties were totally unrestricted. He was the

In a scene from a 1960 film, Huckleberry Finn is pictured with Jim, the runaway slave. Huck defied his upbringing by refusing to turn Jim in to bounty hunters.

only really independent person—boy or man—in the community, and it was by consequence he was tranquilly and continuously happy and was envied by all the rest.[33]

But it was an incident involving Benson Blankenship, Tom's older brother, that gave *The Adventures of Huckleberry Finn* its central plot. Benson, a fisherman, one day found an escaped slave hiding out on Sny Island, across the Mississippi from

Hannibal. Instead of turning the slave in for the substantial monetary reward, Benson Blankenship fed and sheltered the man. The incident had a tragic ending, however. In biographer Andrew Hoffman's words, "Bounty hunters chased the poor slave into a swamp, where he vanished. A few days later, while Sam and some friends were fishing near the island, the slave's body rose to the surface, 'much mutilated' as the local papers reported."[34]

The incident took on profound implications for Sam Clemens. Many years later in his journal, Mark Twain saw Benson Blankenship's decision to harbor a slave as a lesson that "in a crucial situation, a sound heart is a safer guide than an ill-trained conscience." In the novel, Twain uses this notion to support Huck's decision not to turn Jim in to the bounty hunters, asserting that in this instance, "a sound heart and a deformed conscience come into collision and conscience suffers defeat."[35]

Twain goes on to explain the significance of Huck's decision in historical terms:

In those old slave-holding days the whole community was agreed as to one thing—the awful sacredness of slave property. To help steal a horse or a cow was a low crime, but to help a hunted slave . . . or hesitate to promptly betray him to a slave-catcher when the opportunity offered was a much baser crime, and carried with it a stain, a moral smirch which nothing could wipe away.[36]

Mark Twain's Moral Development

Perhaps the greatest difference between the times portrayed in the novel and those during which it was written is that the Civil War had effectively ended slavery in the United States. Nevertheless, the period of Reconstruction during which Twain wrote was at least as problematical for African Americans

as the era of slavery. Racism was still the order of the day, and
no war, no matter how traumatic, could magically solve the
race issue in America. Jim's struggle for freedom and respect
was the plight of most African Americans at the time, and their
trials did not disappear just because the North fought against
the South or because Lincoln signed the Emancipation
Proclamation, or even because the Thirteenth Amendment to
the Constitution abolished slavery.

The development of Mark Twain's attitudes toward race is
as complex as the development of Huck's attitudes. Twain
seemingly never had much stomach for violence toward others, as evidenced by his abortive stay in the Confederate militia and his distaste for duels: "I consider them unwise and I
know that they are dangerous. Also, sinful."[37] In San Francisco
an article he wrote for the *Morning Call* about the brutal beat-
ing of an Asian man was suppressed by its editors.
Nevertheless, as biographer John Lauber suggests, Twain was
not yet open-minded in matters of race:

> He and [his friend Steve] Gillis once amused themselves
> by throwing bottles from their room onto tin roofs of
> Chinese shanties below; reporting he casually referred to
> blacks as "niggers," and he opened one *Call* story with
> "A case of the most infernal description of miscegenation
> [intermarriage between races] has come to light . . . a
> mixture of white and Chinese." But the sight of brutali-
> ty revolted him, and when the impulse moved him, he
> could defy the racial proprieties of his day; an eyewitness
> described him once walking down Montgomery Street
> . . . arm in arm with a black journalist.[38]

Lauber also notes,

> He became aware, over the years, of his attitudes and
> worked to change them, doing his part to pay the debt

that he came to feel every white man owed to every black man. He helped to finance the studies of a black artist in Paris and to pay the way of a black student through Yale Law School; he urged President Garfield to retain the black leader Frederick Douglass as marshal of the District of Columbia; he read and lectured in black churches; in his old age he composed "The United States of Lyncherdom," a searing indictment of the moral cowardice by which the decent majority permitted lynching. . . . Mark Twain became, said his friend William Dean Howells, "the most desouthernized Southerner" that Howells had ever known.[39]

Twain's marriage to Olivia Langdon most likely influenced his beliefs. The Langdons were abolitionists who supported the Underground Railroad. Some of the most prominent members of the antislavery movement—including William Lloyd Garrison, editor of the abolitionist newspaper *The Liberator*; former slave Frederick Douglass; and Gerrit Smith, abolitionist and philanthropist—were guests in the Langdon home, where Livy absorbed their teachings and their liberal attitudes. According to biographer Resa Willis, when Twain was working on *Huckleberry Finn*, Livy told him, "I will give you a motto, & it will be useful to you if you will adopt it: 'Consider every man colored till he is proved white.'"[40]

Imagine then, the added significance in the Twain household of Huck's assertion that "people would call me a lowdown Ablitionist and despise me"[41] for helping Jim to escape to freedom.

In 1985 a Connecticut couple discovered a letter written by Twain that some scholars believe proves to be a final word on the subject of Twain and racism. In the letter, written in 1885, the same year that saw the American publication of *The Adventures of Huckleberry Finn*, Twain offers to provide financial assistance to an African American law student at Yale University. He writes:

I do not believe I would very cheerfully help a white student who would ask a benevolence of a stranger, but I do not feel so about the other color. We have ground the manhood out of them, & the shame is ours, not theirs, & we should pay for it.[42]

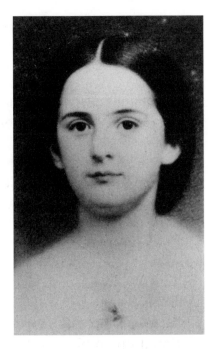

Olivia Langdon Clemens came from a family of abolitionists.

Of the letter and its import, Sterling Stuckey, an African American professor of history at Northwestern University, has said, "It couldn't be a clearer, more categorical indictment of racism in American life and I'm not at all surprised to find that it came from Twain."[43]

A Banned Book

Twain's realistic depiction of life along the Mississippi in the mid–nineteenth century has led to numerous attacks on the novel from the time of its publication to the present. One particularly memorable attack took the form of a ban on the novel by the Concord, Massachusetts, Free Public Library in 1885. The *New York Herald* quoted the now-famous remarks of the Concord Library's Committee members, who said of Twain's novel:

It is couched in the language of a rough ignorant dialect, and all through its pages there is a systematic use of bad grammar and employment of rough, coarse, inelegant expressions. It is also very irreverent. To sum up, the book is flippant and irreverent in its style. It deals with a series of experiences that are certainly not elevating. The whole book is of a class that is more profitable for the slums than it is for respectable people, and it is trash of the veriest sort.[44]

The debate over *Huckleberry Finn* was only beginning. While many saw the book as a powerful antislavery novel, others could not get past Huck's lying and stealing to see through to his essential morality.

In the late twentieth century, the debate took on a new form as many readers, especially some African Americans, began to react against the racial epithet "nigger" flung around so cavalierly by the pre–Civil War white characters of the novel. One school administrator, John Wallace, in a widely reprinted op-ed piece, echoes the opinion of the Concord Library Committee, when he begins his essay by saying that the novel "is the most grotesque example of racist trash ever written."[45]

With this new controversy, often based around a single offensive word, the novel began to be banned with increasing regularity. School districts around the country began to remove the novel from their libraries and their required reading lists, "claiming that such language damaged the self-esteem of young African Americans."[46]

Recognizing the merits as well as the dangers of teaching *The Adventures of Huckleberry Finn*, some school districts, such as that in Cherry Hill, New Jersey, installed new programs to save the novel by placing it within its historical context and teaching it in units that included other important books on the history of African Americans in the United States, such as Frederick Douglass's *Narrative of the Life of Frederick Douglass*, and Harriet Jacobs's *Incidents in the Life of a Slave Girl*.

But for as long as *Huckleberry Finn* continues to be read, it will seemingly cause controversy. And it is not a book that can be lightly dismissed. In the words of one Twain expert, David Bradley, "You can't arbitrarily say this book is trouble, we're not going to teach it, because a book like *Huckleberry Finn* is part of American literature. You can't get around it."[47]

CHAPTER THREE

The Plot

A t the outset of the story, Huckleberry Finn introduces himself as the narrator of the book and describes how he starred in Mark Twain's previous novel *The Adventures of Tom Sawyer*. Huck and his friend Tom Sawyer had discovered a pirates' stash at the end of that book, and Huck had come away with $6,000. The Widow Douglas has taken the former street urchin into her home, hoping to "sivilize" him. When the widow's sister, Miss Watson, comes to live with them, she immediately applies her no-nonsense educational tactics to Huck. Miss Watson allows Huck little freedom and constantly chides him for minor offenses such as yawning or not sitting still.

Tom Sawyer's Gang

One night Huck hears Tom Sawyer's signal, "me-yow," outside his window, so he climbs down to the ground and joins his friend. The two play a practical joke on Miss Watson's slave, Jim, who is dozing beneath a tree. They hang his hat on a branch above him, and Jim later awakens, sees the hat in the tree, and surmises that he has been the victim of a spell placed on him by witches.

Soon after, Tom and Huck meet up with a group of boys including Jo Harper and Ben Rogers. They agree to form a "band of robbers" called Tom Sawyer's Gang. Led by Tom, who bases all of his often naïve opinions on adventure stories he has read, the boys discuss how they will engage in make-believe activities such as robbing, kidnapping, and ransoming their victims. The boys return home by morning.

Three or four months pass as fall turns into winter. Huck has attended school, learning the basics of spelling, reading, writing, and mathematics. Huck's father, Pap, has not been seen for a year. When a corpse is found floating in the Mississippi, some conjecture that it is Huck's dead father. But Huck is convinced that his father is still alive.

One day he spies a distinctive footprint in the newly fallen snow and realizes that his father is back in town. Fearful that Pap has come to town to claim Huck's $6,000, Huck hurries over to Judge Thatcher's house in an attempt to convince the judge to keep the money, which the judge has been holding for Huck. When the judge wonders why, Huck will not answer. The judge gives Huck a dollar for his troubles.

Still worried, Huck hurries to Miss Watson's slave, Jim, to have his future read by Jim's fortune-telling device, "a hairball as big as your fist." But Jim offers only a generic fortune

A scene from a 1939 film shows Huck with the goodhearted but misguided Widow Douglas (right) and her sister, Miss Watson.

to Huck, who pays him with a counterfeit quarter. When Huck returns to his room, his worst fears are confirmed: "There set Pap, his own self."[48]

Kidnapped by Pap

Pap is almost fifty years old, a derelict with long greasy hair who is dressed in "just rags, that was all." He has learned of Huck's riches and is displeased that his son is being educated. Pap takes Huck's dollar and turns up drunk at Judge Thatcher's house the next day, demanding Huck's fortune, to no avail. So Pap kidnaps his son and takes him across the Mississippi River to Illinois, where he has found a deserted log hut. At first Huck is happy to return to nature, but he soon grows tired of Pap's abusive treatment and devises an elaborate plan to fake his own death and escape. One night Pap awakens Huck, whom he mistakes for "the Angel of Death,"[49] and chases the poor boy around the cabin with a knife. Before he can harm Huck, he once again falls asleep in a drunken stupor.

The next day the two go out in search of food, and Huck finds a canoe and, later that day, a nine-log raft, floating downriver. He hides the canoe, but Pap takes the raft, which he can sell in town for money to buy more whiskey. As soon as Pap leaves, Huck prepares to fake his own death. He wants those who arrive at the scene to believe that robbers have killed him and dumped his body in the river, so he spreads pig's blood on the cabin floor and drags a bag of rocks down to the river and dumps it in.

Huck paddles the canoe to Jackson's Island in the middle of the Mississippi, a few miles downriver from Hannibal. For several days he lives peacefully, smoking his pipe and feasting on Mississippi River catfish. But one day he comes across a newly extinguished campfire. Nearby, he discovers Miss Watson's slave, Jim, who has also taken refuge on the island upon learning that Miss Watson has contemplated selling him downriver to New Orleans. Jim is horrified at seeing what he

Huck, pictured here with his abusive father, Pap, thinks up an ingenious plan to escape the evil man's wrath.

believes is Huck's ghost, but Huck soon convinces Jim that he is not dead. Though it makes Huck feel "like a low-down Ablitionist,"[50] he promises not to inform others about his fellow runaway.

Jim and Huck spend their days exploring, hunting, and lazing around. One night they spy a two-story houseboat floating downriver. Once inside, they discover a dead man lying facedown. Jim warns Huck not to look at the man because the sight is too ghastly. They return to camp.

Escaping Down the Mississippi

Huck grows bored with life on the island and offers to go to shore to learn if there is any news circulating about Huck's "death" and Jim's escape. Huck disguises himself in girls' clothing and goes to the house of Mrs. Judith Loftus, a newcomer to town. Mrs. Loftus informs Huck that Pap was initially under suspicion for murdering Huck, but when the townspeople learned Jim was gone, he became the primary suspect. There is a $300 reward for Jim's capture, she says, and several citizens are eager to claim it. Informing Huck that she has recently seen smoke on Jackson's Island, Mrs. Loftus confides that her husband and another man are going over there that very night. Throughout their talk, the shrewd Mrs. Loftus suspects that Huck is not a girl. When she guesses that he is really a runaway apprentice, Huck goes along with her story. The good-hearted Mrs. Loftus warns him to be careful and to ask for her if he gets in trouble. Huck leaves, then hurries back to the island to warn Jim: "There ain't a minute to lose. They're after us."[51]

The pair head downriver, taking both the canoe and a raft they had found. Aided by good weather, they follow the current by night and rest by day. Five nights below St. Louis a fierce storm strikes, and Huck and Jim take shelter beneath a makeshift wigwam that Jim has constructed on the raft. In the glare of the storm's lightning, Huck sees a steamboat, the *Walter Scott*, that has "killed herself" on the rocks in the middle of the river. Despite Jim's protests, they board the wrecked ship, looking for plunder. But they soon realize that they are in the company of three murderers, one of whom has been tied up by the other two, who plan to leave him on board to drown as the ship breaks apart. Huck and Jim steal the skiff

After finding a raft by chance, Huck and Jim make their escape down the Mississippi River.

the two thieves plan to use in their getaway, leaving all three cutthroats in a perilous situation. But Huck's conscience gnaws at him. Spotting a night watchman along the shore, Huck persuades the man to go rescue those on board the *Walter Scott*. But it is already too late, and Huck sees its wreckage washing downriver.

Sailing Past Cairo

Huck and Jim form a plan to raft downriver until reaching Cairo, Illinois, where the Ohio River joins the Mississippi.

There they can take passage on a steamboat bound for the free states. Before they can enact their plan, a dense fog settles over the river and the two are separated, with Jim still on the raft and Huck in the canoe. Huck feverishly tries to locate Jim in the fog. But when an island in the river separates them, Huck loses hope. Giving up, he falls asleep.

When Huck wakes, the night is bright with stars overhead. He finally locates the raft up ahead and finds Jim asleep on it. Huck tricks Jim into believing there was never any fog and that Jim had dreamed the entire episode. When Jim realizes Huck's deception, he is severely disappointed to have been played for a fool. He lets Huck know, and Huck gives his friend a sincere apology.

As the two continue down the river, Jim's mood picks up. He plans to escape to a free state, save every cent he can, then buy his wife and children out of slavery. Jim's scheme alarms Huck, who has been raised in a slave state. Believing he has stolen Jim from Miss Watson, he reconsiders his decision to help Jim run away. Huck's crisis of conscience leads him to resolve to turn Jim in immediately. But as he is leaving the raft, Jim calls after him, shouting that "de ole true Huck" is the only white man who ever kept his promise to Jim.

Moments later two bounty hunters confront Huck. They are searching for escaped slaves and demand to know who is on the raft that Huck has just left. Huck assures them that it is a white man, but the two are suspicious until Huck invents a story about how his father, a victim of smallpox, is on the raft and needs assistance. Immediately the men—fearing the deadly disease—lose interest and leave. Huck feels guilty over lying; he believes he's done wrong. Then he realizes that he would have felt no better if he *had* turned Jim in.

The two resume their journey, still searching for Cairo, but eventually it dawns on them that they must have passed it the previous night in the fog. More bad luck strikes as they lose their canoe and cannot paddle back upriver to Cairo. Back on the raft

The friendship and trust between Huck and Jim deepens as they surmount obstacles together.

that night, they set off to buy a canoe along the shore. A malicious steamboat captain, however, ruins their plans. He steers his huge craft right through their raft, and both jump overboard in the nick of time. In the confusion and churning waters caused by the steamboat, Huck and Jim are separated again.

The Grangerfords and the Shepherdsons

Huck swims ashore and is discovered by the Grangerfords, an aristocratic southern family locked in a feud with their neighbors, the Shepherdsons. The family takes him into their home and treats him with kindness. Heading the family is Colonel Grangerford, a tall thin "gentleman" with "the blackest kind of eyes."[52] His family includes his wife; their adult children, Bob, Tom, Miss Charlotte, and Miss Sophia; and Buck, who is Huck's age.

One day while hunting in the woods, Huck is surprised to see Buck take a shot at Harney Shepherdson. In this manner, Huck is indoctrinated into the long-running feud. The next Sunday, the family attends church, where they hear a sermon on brotherly love. Later that day the slave assigned to Huck leads him to a spot along the river where Huck is astonished to find Jim, alive and well. After a conversation during which Jim reveals that he has been fixing their raft, Huck returns to the Grangerford house.

The next day Huck wakes to learn that Miss Sophia has eloped with Harney Shepherdson, and the feud has resumed with a vengeance. Colonel Grangerford and two of his sons have been killed, along with "two or three" of the Shepherdsons. Not long after, Buck is shot to death by the Shepherdsons, and a tearful Huck escapes back to the river and Jim.

The King and the Duke

Huck and Jim continue their journey south. One day Huck finds a canoe and paddles to the shore, where he sees two slovenly men—one about thirty years old, the other seventy—running for their lives from a pack of men and dogs. Huck aids in their escape by paddling them out of sight in the canoe. The younger man has been selling medicine that cleans teeth but also strips off the enamel; the older man has been running a temperance, or antidrinking, revival but was discovered one night with a jug of alcohol. Once they are no longer in danger, the two men decide they will become a team. The younger man insists he is the deposed Duke of Bridgewater. When the elder man observes the royal treatment Huck and Jim give to the "duke," he declares that he is the rightful descendant of a line of French kings. Huck easily sees through this deception, but he says nothing, preferring to put up with their lies rather than stir up trouble. When the con men inquire as to whether Jim is a runaway slave, Huck concocts a tale of his own to convince them that his family owns Jim.

The king, duke, and Huck go ashore at Pokeville, a "little one-horse town" that is nearly empty due to a camp meeting in the woods. The duke finds a printer's shop that has been left unattended and, acting as if he were the proprietor, takes orders from customers who enter the shop and keeps the money for himself. Meanwhile the king and Huck go to the camp meeting, a religious revival attended by a

After rescuing the duke (left) and the king (center), Huck realizes that they are con men.

thousand people. The king pretends he is a former pirate, who, having seen the error of his ways, plans to reform other pirates. He then implores the crowd for money to support his cause. So convincing is the aged con man, that he collects over $87 from his dupes.

With their pockets full, the king and duke return to the raft with Huck and Jim and devise another moneymaking scheme. They plan to imitate renowned English actors and perform Shakespearean scenes in the next town they come to. Once they reach Arkansas, they go ashore at another small dilapidated town. Huck describes loafers chewing tobacco on the storefront porches and pigs lazing in the muddy streets. Into this scene comes the town drunk, Boggs, who stops in front of a store and begins loudly abusing Colonel Sherburn, who, he claims, has swindled him. The colonel emerges from the building, warning Boggs that he will put up with the abuse for only so long. When the drunken but essentially harmless Boggs continues his tirade, Sherburn shoots Boggs dead. The townspeople plan to lynch Sherburn for his crime, but when they assemble outside Sherburn's door, he launches into a tirade and calls them cowards because they can only act as a mob but not confront him individually. Defeated, the would-be lynch mob disperses.

That night the king and duke put on their performance, but only twelve people show up to see their scenes from Shakespeare. The duke schedules a new performance, "The Royal Nonesuch," printing up signs for this act with the prominent notice: LADIES AND CHILDREN NOT ADMITTED. As he suspects, there is a packed house for the evening's performance. The entire show consists of the king prancing around completely naked, his body painted with rainbow stripes. The audience howls with laughter until they realize that they've been taken: the show only lasts for a few minutes. They are ready to do the king and duke harm until one man suggests that they will be the laughingstocks of the town if others find out they have been so easily duped. He suggests they tell the rest of the town what a great show "Nonesuch" is, and, sure enough, on the second evening there is another packed house. On the third evening the makeshift theater is packed once more, this time by previous audience members who have stuffed their pockets with rotten vegetables and eggs. But before they have a chance to vent their fury on the king and duke, the two rascals are already back on the raft sailing downriver with Huck and Jim, having duped the townspeople for $465 in the three nights. Jim is shocked at the low morals of these royals, but Huck assures him that most kings are even worse.

The Wilks Affair

Back onshore the king meets a young man waiting to take a steamboat for New Orleans and devises a new plan. Pumping the young country "jake" for information, he learns that a man named Peter Wilks has recently passed away, leaving a substantial estate. The man's brothers—Harvey, a preacher, and William, who is "deef and dumb"—are en route from Sheffield, England, and expected any day. The king immediately hatches a plan to impersonate Harvey and have the duke play the role of William, in order to bilk the heirs, Peter's three daughters, of their $6,000 inheritance.

Arriving at the village, the phony Wilks brothers and Huck meet Peter's three teenage daughters, Mary Jane, Susan, and Joanna. The girls, now orphaned, are delighted to see their uncles and completely taken in by the ruse, despite the king's absurd English accent and the duke's use of baby talk, "Goo goo—goo-goo-goo," to play a hearing-impaired man. The Wilkses' old friend Dr. Robinson is the only person not fooled by the king and duke. But when he insists that they are fakers, the naïve Mary Jane declares her loyalty toward her "uncles." She gives them the $6,000 for safekeeping as a show of her belief in them.

The duke and the king attempt to defraud Mary Jane Wilks (pictured) and her sisters of their inheritance by impersonating the brothers of her deceased father.

Huck feels guilty over deceiving such sweet girls and steals the $6,000 from the king and duke. He hides the money in Peter Wilks's open casket in the parlor. After the funeral, the king and duke realize their horde of money is missing and accost Huck, who slyly suggests that he had earlier seen several slaves tiptoeing out of the king and duke's room.

The next morning Huck tells Mary Jane her "uncles" are frauds. He makes her promise that she will go stay with some friends so as not to immediately expose the con men. He is worried that any difficult situation may place Jim in danger.

That afternoon another set of brothers arrives in the village claiming to be William and Harvey. Their appearance sets the town in an uproar. But the townspeople cannot verify the legitimacy of either set of brothers until the new Harvey reveals that his deceased brother had a tattoo on his chest.

Both the king and Harvey offer plausible descriptions of the dead man's tattoo. With no other way to ascertain the truth, the cry goes out to dig up the grave. The townspeople rush to the cemetery. When the grave is unearthed, the mob discovers the bag of gold Huck had hidden in the coffin, and chaos ensues. In the confusion, Huck escapes.

Back on the raft, Huck and Jim start downriver, but to their dismay, the king and duke accost them. They too had escaped in the confusion. Each man suspects the other of having hidden the gold in the coffin. Angered, the younger and stronger duke viciously chokes the king. Though he did not steal the gold, the king admits to the deed to avoid the duke's further wrath.

The four continue their journey down the Mississippi for many days until the con men once again feel safe and venture out to river towns to perform their specialties. But their new schemes are largely unsuccessful, and Huck fears they will soon resort to burglary or other crimes. He wants to escape from these dangerous men as soon as possible. One morning they dock near the town of Pikesville, and the king goes off to see if the locals have heard of "The Royal Nonesuch," which he wants to try once again. Eventually, Huck and the duke find the drunken old man in a tavern, the duke argues with him, and Huck seizes the opportunity to slip away. When he returns to the raft, Jim is gone.

The Phelps Plantation

A boy informs Huck that an old man sold a runaway slave to Silas Phelps, owner of a nearby plantation. For once, Huck does not know what to do. He believes he has been sinful for enabling Jim's escape. He writes a letter to Miss Watson in the belief that he will be cleansed of sin for telling the truth. Upon finishing the letter, Huck has second thoughts. With the words, "All right, then, I'll *go* to hell,"[53] he tears up the letter and resolves to steal Jim out of slavery.

Huck arrives at the Phelps plantation and is warmly greeted by Mrs. Sally Phelps. She mistakes Huck for her nephew

Having been reared to believe that slavery is normal, Huck is dubious about helping Jim to escape, but his heart will not let him betray his friend.

Tom, who has been expected for days. Huck is perplexed until she introduces him to her husband as Tom Sawyer. When Huck hears a steamboat whistle, he realizes that the real Tom may show up any minute, and he must find him first so that Tom won't expose him. He heads for town, and, sure enough, meets Tom Sawyer coming the other way. Believing Huck to have been murdered, Tom thinks he is seeing a ghost. Huck soon convinces Tom that he is, indeed, alive. He informs Tom of the situation, and the ever-scheming Tom is happy to go along with Huck's ruse. What really surprises Huck is that Tom is also willing to help free Jim. Ironically, Huck's good opinion of Tom is lessened considerably by Tom's immoral intentions. An upstanding young man would not help free a slave, Huck believes.

Tom shows up at the Phelps plantation claiming to be Sid Sawyer, also visiting from up north. That night one of the Phelps children asks to go to the show that is to be put on by the king and duke, but Mr. Phelps says that it has been canceled. The captured slave has revealed the truth about the con men running the show. Knowing that the king and duke are in dire trouble, Huck takes Tom out to warn them. But it is too late. The king and duke have been tarred and feathered and ridden out of town. Despite all the king and duke have done, Huck feels sorry for them.

Tom and Huck find Jim locked up in a ramshackle hut. Freeing Jim seems easy, but each time Huck suggests a plan, Tom asserts that it is too simple. He believes that escapes should be daring and complex, like those in the adventure novels he has read. The next morning the boys visit Jim's hut, and Tom assures Jim, "We're going to set you free."[54] But Tom sets about inventing numerous ways to make Jim's escape more difficult.

The boys use picks and shovels to tunnel into Jim's hut. But instead of immediately helping Jim to escape, Tom explains his elaborate plan to Jim, in which the runaway slave will be transformed into the unfairly imprisoned hero of a romance novel. They will eventually get Jim out, he says, but first they must do things by the book. Trusting in the boys, Jim abides by their convoluted scheme. Their efforts to "free" Jim continue for weeks.

Meanwhile Mr. Phelps has not been able to find the run-away slave's owner, so he decides to advertise in the New Orleans and St. Louis newspapers. This alarms Huck, and Tom agrees to hurry his plan along. According to Tom, they must inform the Phelpses of the impending escape. They leave a series of ominous warnings that Jim will be freed by a gang, until the Phelps household is in a frenzied state. On the night of the escape, Huck and Tom awaken at 11:30 to find that a mob of farmers with guns has gathered downstairs. Huck is fearful of such firepower, and the boys dash to Jim's hut. Just as they are escaping, the armed farmers crowd into the dark-ened hut. Tom's pants catch on a splinter while he is climbing a fence and the noise alarms the farmers, who hurry after them. Shots are fired. Tom, Huck, and Jim make it to the raft and are about to set off down the river, when they discover that Tom has been shot in the calf. Despite Tom's protests, Jim insists that they get a doctor.

A Happy Ending

Two days later Tom is carried home to the Phelpses' house on a mattress, accompanied by a doctor and Jim, who is in chains. Jim is verbally and physically abused by the townspeople as a runaway slave until the kindly doctor explains how loyally Jim stayed by Tom.

Tom awakens the morning after feeling much better and proudly confesses the entire affair to Aunt Sally. He is sur-prised to learn that Jim has been captured and insists he must be set free. When Aunt Sally questions this preposterous idea, Tom reveals another secret: Miss Watson had died two months before and had been so ashamed of keeping a slave that she freed Jim in her will.

At this point Tom's Aunt Polly appears in the door. Polly has journeyed over a thousand miles downriver in an attempt to learn just what tricks Tom has been up to. Tom admits that he had intercepted letters that she had written to her sister

Sally, knowing they would pose a problem. Aunt Polly reveals the true identities of the boys to her thoroughly bewildered sister and confirms Tom's assertion that Jim is free.

As Huck's tale draws to its conclusion, there is one last surprise. Huck believes that by now Pap must have claimed his $6,000, but Tom assures him it is still safe. Jim reveals that Pap was the dead man on the houseboat whose face he would not let Huck see. Tom gives Jim $40 for all of his troubles during the escape.

Aunt Sally intends to adopt Huck, but Huck decides that he will instead "light out for the [Indian] territory,"[55] because as far as "sivilization" goes, he's been there before.

CHAPTER FOUR

The Cast of Characters

The Widow Douglas

The Widow Douglas is a St. Petersburg woman who takes Huck into her home in order to teach him the respectability expected of a boy worth $6,000. She treats Huck well, and while she is disappointed by his lapses, she is never harsh.

The Duke

The duke is the younger of two confidence men who run into Jim and Huck while fleeing from a mob of their dupes. He is a man skilled in numerous forms of deception and often uses his knowledge of printing to make posters or flyers to further his schemes. Prior to meeting the king, Huck, and Jim, he had been selling a concoction to take tartar off the teeth, though, unfortunately, it removes the enamel with it. His other cons include lecturing, teaching singing-geography school, and practicing mesmerism (hypnotism) and phrenology (studying the bumps on skulls).

The duke concocts "The Royal Nonesuch" and gets the king to be the true buffoon of that act. The duke is the physically stronger and more intimidating of the pair, cowing the older king after they fail to steal a fortune from the Wilks sisters. At times he is more conservative in his schemes and slightly less absurd than his companion, the king. He wants to escape from the Wilks sisters with just their gold, while the king wants the money from their possessions and home as well.

Huckleberry Finn

Huck is the protagonist of the novel, a thirteen-year-old urchin whose mother is dead and whose father is the town drunk. Good-hearted, street-smart, and mischievous, Huck has been adopted by the Widow Douglas after he helped to rescue her from the evil Injun Joe in Twain's earlier novel, *Tom Sawyer*. But the widow's sister, Miss Watson, has made life hard on Huck with her continual prodding to act more

Although mischievous, Huck is a wise and kindhearted boy, full of pluck and resourcefulness.

civilized. Huck despises "sivilization" and all that comes with it. He longs for his former freedom, when he could dress in rags and live in the woods, even if it means putting up with the abusive ways of Pap, who returns to town to claim Huck's money.

Perhaps Huck's most useful trait is his ability to extricate himself from a difficult situation through an elaborate tale or lie. Once he begins his journey with the slave Jim, Huck is always ready with a story, often plausible, to save Jim or to further their quest downriver. He lies to almost every other character in the book at one time or another, though his lies are often necessary for survival.

As street-smart as Huck usually is, when Tom Sawyer is around, both at the beginning and the end of the book, Huck can be quite gullible. He abides by all that Tom Sawyer says and often does not want to realize that Tom is playing "pretend" until, as in the case of Jim's escape from the Phelps plantation, it is too late.

As an impressionable boy living in a slave state, Missouri, before the Civil War, Huck has no problem with the institution of slavery or its cardinal belief that blacks are inferior to whites. Therefore, when he is faced with a situation in which he must aid and abet a fugitive slave, his first impulse is not to be a "low-down Ablitionist." Nevertheless, Huck's good nature and his common sense often prevail over society's rules, causing Huck to stop short every time he comes close to informing on his new friend and surrogate father.

Even so, Huck maintains much of society's harmful beliefs right to the end of the book. When, late in the novel, Tom's Aunt Sally asks Huck if anyone was hurt in a steamboat explosion, Huck replies, "No'm killed a nigger."[56] This response indicates that despite all that Huck has learned from traveling with a black man, he still cannot shed his ingrained racist beliefs. He is a complex character, and he exhibits human faults, making him more realistic to readers.

Though Huck had returned to the Widow Douglas's house after running away in chapter 1 for the express purpose of joining Tom Sawyer's Gang, Huck is never able to adapt to civilization. At the end of the novel, when Aunt Sally wishes to adopt and civilize the nomadic Huck, he reports that he will head out to Indian territory because he's tried civilization before, and it certainly isn't for him.

Pap Finn

Huckleberry Finn's alcoholic, bigoted, brutal father returns to St. Petersburg shortly after the novel begins in the hopes of stealing his son's newfound wealth. He kidnaps Huck and takes him to a deserted cabin on the Illinois side of the river. Pap locks Huck up during the day while he goes to town to get drunk. On one particularly horrific night, he chases Huck around the cabin with a knife, calling the boy "the Angel of Death" and attempting to kill him. Pap does not survive the novel, however. Huck and Jim discover his corpse in an abandoned houseboat. Jim is the first to see the body and hides its identity from Huck, telling Huck not to look at the face because it is too ghastly. Only at the end of the novel does Jim reveal the truth.

The Grangerfords

This aristocratic family takes Huck in when he swims ashore after his raft has been demolished by a steamboat. The head of the family is Colonel Grangerford, who has seen his family suffer greatly due to their blood feud with the Shepherdsons. Huck is mightily impressed with the colonel's noble appearance, but he is exposed as a patriarch willing to see his sons die rather than end the senseless feud that has continued for generations to the point where the younger members of the clan do not understand why they are fighting.

Other members of the family are his wife; their adult children Bob, Tom, Miss Charlotte, and Miss Sophia; and their son Buck, who is Huck's age. Buck befriends Huck in the guise of George Jackson when he turns up at their plantation. Buck is a good-natured, friendly, generous boy who nevertheless wholeheartedly embraces the violence of the feud. Huck is saddened at his friend's death when Buck and another boy are cornered and shot down by older Shepherdsons.

Jim

Jim is a rather unlikely figure around which to construct the plot of a novel. Part two-dimensional stereotype, part fully realized, profound, sensitive, and strong father figure and hero, Jim is, in the words of critic Bernard W. Bell, "the best example of the humanity of black American slaves in nineteenth-century white American fiction."[57]

Jim's dilemma becomes the central focus of the novel. When Huck finds him on Jackson's Island, Jim has escaped from Miss Watson, his owner, because he has heard that she has decided to sell him down the river, where he will have to endure the harsh life of a plantation slave in Louisiana. Huck's decision to aid in Jim's escape provides the impetus for the novel's plot and for Twain's commentary on slavery and racism.

Jim's genuine love and compassion for Huck, and for children in general, comes through often in Twain's portrayal. He protects Huck from seeing his dead father in the houseboat. He laments a time when he punished his own daughter for not listening to him, unaware that scarlet fever had made her deaf. And at the end of the novel, when Jim has a chance to escape from the Phelps plantation, he instead nurses the wounded Tom at his own peril.

Jim is also a comic figure. He is highly superstitious (as is Huck), believing that snakeskins cause calamity and blaming unexplained troubles on witches. But he can also employ superstition for his own benefit, as when he uses a "hair-ball" to predict the future and obtain money from those soliciting its advice.

Mark Twain uses Jim's plight to illuminate the injustice of slavery.

Huck does not always treat Jim well, teasing him and playing practical jokes at the same time as he helps Jim to run away. But Jim's dignity emerges more clearly each time he is placed in an undignified or adverse situation. In one such instance, Huck returns to the raft after the two have been separated on the river by a dense fog. He attempts to trick Jim into believing that their long and fearful separation was only a bad dream. When Jim catches on to the nature of Huck's prank, he scolds the boy, telling Huck that he had been heart-broken over almost losing Huck for good. Huck realizes he has wronged a friend and apologizes to Jim.

The King

The king is the older of the two con men whom Huck and Jim befriend. He is in his seventies with a bald head and "very grey whiskers." Before hooking up with the duke, Huck, and Jim, he had been running a temperance, or antidrinking revival, but was caught with "a private jug on the sly."[58] The king is often an absurd figure, as when, naked and painted, he prances

The scheming king and duke reward Huck's kindness by continually present-ing the boy with moral dilemmas.

around on all fours during "The Royal Nonesuch" or plays Juliet in a full beard during their presentation of scenes from Shakespeare. The king is often even less principled than his partner in crime. It is he who tries to push the Wilks scheme for every last cent, and he ultimately betrays Huck and Jim by selling Jim back into slavery.

Sally Phelps

Sally Phelps is a sweet, generous, and loving aunt of Tom Sawyer who lives on an extensive farm in southern Arkansas. Aunt Sally is thoroughly confused by the antics of Tom and Huck. Many times she is driven to punish the boys with a spanking, but she is often far less harsh than she might be and they do not take her discipline seriously. At the conclusion of the novel, Aunt Sally wishes to adopt Huck.

Silas Phelps

Silas is Tom Sawyer's uncle and the benevolent husband of Aunt Sally. His kindness even extends to the captured slave, Jim. He prays with Jim and makes sure that he is well fed. Like his wife, Silas is completely dumbfounded by the ongoing events on the plantation once Huck and Tom arrive.

Aunt Polly

Aunt Polly is Tom's guardian. She is a strict, no-nonsense child-rearer with a heart, who has trouble keeping up with Tom's shenanigans. Polly appears only in the very last scene of the novel, when, worried about not receiving letters from Sally which Tom has intercepted, she journeys to the Phelps plantation. Polly's identification of Huck and Tom helps to clear up her sister's confusion.

Tom Sawyer

Huck's pal, Tom Sawyer, is a mischievous thirteen-year-old who lives in a dream world of romantic adventures he has learned about through a voracious appetite for romance novels. Tom is a natural leader who uses his influence to draw the other boys into acting out wild schemes he has read about. He often refers to the books he has read to prove to the other boys his schemes are legitimate.

Early in the novel Tom organizes his schoolmates into a band of robbers who will act out these adventures in various criminal activities, including kidnapping. But the plan is sabotaged when no one in the group knows what "ransom" means.

Tom is a "respectable" boy, in Huck's eyes. He lives with his Aunt Polly and attends school, though he will often play hooky or climb out his window late at night to round up the other boys for adventures. He has never met a practical joke he didn't like, and this love rubs off on Huck.

Late in the novel, Huck is shocked when a respectable boy such as Tom agrees to help free Jim from the Phelps plantation, since freeing a slave was considered a despicable act. Huck appreciates the help but his esteem for Tom is lowered. Yet, in the end, Tom reveals that Jim had been legally free for some time and that their act of liberation was just that—an act.

The Shepherdsons

This Arkansas clan is made up of "five or six" families. They share the same steamboat landing with the Grangerfords, their archrivals. Harney Shepherdson, whom Huck describes as a "splendid young man,"[59] falls in love with Sophia Grangerford. Their late-night elopement leads to the fierce battle in which Buck Grangerford and his two brothers are killed.

Judge Thatcher

The judge is a kind man who looks after Huck's fortune. When Huck's father, Pap, returns to town after hearing of his son's wealth, Judge Thatcher attempts to keep him from claiming guardianship of Huck. But his attempt fails when another judge, new to town and naïve to Pap's true character, rules against them.

Miss Watson

Miss Watson is the Widow Douglas's sister, and together they are Huck's chief antagonists as the novel opens. Miss Watson is a constant fault-finder, demanding that Huck conform to her rules. She tries to teach Huck about religion and prayer, but she is scandalized when he says that he would rather go to hell than heaven if she is going to heaven.

The Wilks Sisters

The three teenaged Wilks sisters, Mary Jane, Susan, and Joanna, have been orphaned following the death of their father, Peter Wilks. As the eldest, Mary Jane is the leader, a sweet and gullible, yet strong-willed young woman. She naïvely trusts the king and duke, who pretend to be her uncles from England. When Joanna, whom Huck refers to as "hair-lip," nearly exposes Huck for a fraud after she catches him in numerous contradictions concerning his supposed hometown of Sheffield, England, the good-hearted Mary Jane makes her apologize to Huck. She continues to trust the king and duke despite the wise counsel of Dr. Robinson, a family friend. When Huck finally takes Mary Jane into his confidence and reveals the truth about the two con men, she willingly goes along with Huck's plan, listening to his advice to bide her time before exposing the two "rapscallions." Huck is quite taken with Mary Jane and believes her to have more "sand" than any young woman he has known.

CHAPTER FIVE

Literary Analysis

*T*heAdventures of Huckleberry Finn is a novel about America. As such, its themes and concerns are often those that run throughout the American novel. One reason that *The Adventures of Huckleberry Finn* continues to be relevant into the twenty-first century is because Twain tackles many of the major concerns of daily American life, including social class distinctions, racism, and good and evil.

Commentary on Social Class

In *The Adventures of Huckleberry Finn* Twain presents a cross section of American society in the 1830s. The slaves are represented in particular by Jim. Huck and his father are lower-class illiterates. Tom Sawyer, his aunt, the Widow Douglas, and Miss Watson are all drawn from the middle class. The Shepherdsons and Grangerfords represent the wealthy, aristocratic upper class. Finally, Twain throws in a mock king and duke. Twain inverts the social hierarchy so that those who claim social status are often absurd and those who are of the lowest class end up as the most truly noble.

In general, Twain is scornful of the class structure and pretensions to superiority. Such scorn emerges in Huck's naïve description of Colonel Grangerford:

> Col. Grangerford was a gentleman, you see. He was a
> gentleman all over; and so was his family. He was well

born, as the saying is, and that's worth as much in a man as it is in a horse, so the Widow Douglas said, and nobody ever denied that she was of the first aristocracy in our town; and pap he always said it, too, though he warn't no more quality than a mud-cat himself.[60]

Huck has been taught that class counts. If one is wellborn, one's essential goodness is beyond reproach. But Twain plays off Huck's naïveté to present the reader with an entirely different message. The colonel, for all of his civility, is engaged in a brutal ongoing battle with a neighboring, equally aristocratic family, the Shepherdsons. Their feud brings them closer to savages than to civilized people. Huck cannot understand this because he has been brainwashed about the importance of class, but he knows something is dreadfully wrong with these supposedly admirable people.

Twain also has much fun with monarchy in the form of the two pretenders, the king and the duke. A major theme in many of his other works—*The Prince and The Pauper*, *Pudd'nhead Wilson*, and *A Connecticut Yankee in King Arthur's Court*, among the more popular manifestations—is that being "well born" does not make one any more noble. Though such men claim noble titles, their actions are crude and base. Huck understands that many true monarchs act similarly. Twain suggests that true nobility is demonstrated, not claimed, in passages such as the following dialogue between Jim and Huck:

"Don't it sprise you de way dem kings carries on, Huck?"

"No," I says, "it don't."

"Why don't it, Huck?"

"Well, it don't, because it's in the breed. I reckon they're all alike."

"But, Huck, dese kings o' ourn is reglar rapscallions; dat's jist what dey is; dey's reglar rapscallions."

"Well, that's what I'm a-saying; all kings is mostly rapscallions, as fur as I can make out."[61]

Huck goes on to give a fractured, hilariously butchered version of the history of monarchy; nevertheless, his and Twain's essential message comes through at the end: "All I say is, kings is kings, and you got to make allowances. Take them all around, they're a mighty ornery lot. It's the way they're raised."[62]

Americans, of course, rejected the concept of monarchy as a basis for the founding of the United States of America in 1776. Twain's criticism of royalty stems in part from such ideology. But politics aside, Twain favors inner goodness over social graces. Not surprisingly, his two heroes are drawn from the lowest strata of society. Huck is a poor white and Jim a slave. Huck has his own flaws: He rarely tells the truth, he steals, and he is gullible, particularly when it comes to superstition. But when faced with a dire situation, Huck usually does the right thing. Thus he supports Jim's escape down the Mississippi, attempts to save the cutthroats trapped on the *Walter Scott*, and turns against the king and duke when their schemes threaten to ruin the lives of the Wilks sisters.

Twain casts Jim in a similar light. Despite his ignorance, superstitions, and downright foolishness, Jim emerges as the novel's most moral, dependable, worthy, and admirable character. It is an irony that is sheer Twain, for in the nineteenth-century American South, there was no class lower than slaves. As Shelley Fisher Fishkin writes, "Mark Twain knew that there was nothing, absolutely *nothing*, a black man could do—including selflessly sacrificing his freedom, the only thing of value he had—that would make white society see beyond the color of his skin."[63] Jim's worthiness is nowhere more apparent than at the novel's end, where he has the chance to run off and save himself but instead steadfastly nurses Tom Sawyer, the same Tom Sawyer who has, however innocently, abused him for weeks with his idiotic prison games.

Civilization Versus Nature

"Sivilization" may be Huck's ignorant misspelling, but it is also Twain's metaphor for a society that is often more savage than civilized. As the novel begins, the Widow Douglas and her sister, Miss Watson, undertake the task of "sivilizing" Huck: "The widow Douglas, she took me for her son, and allowed she would sivilize me; but it was rough living in the house all the time, considering how dismal regular and decent the widow was in all her ways"; Huck equates "sivilization" with discomfort and boredom. He must sit for long periods of time, without moving or even yawning: "Don't gap and stretch like that, Huckleberry—why don't you try to behave?"[64] Miss Watson scolds.

For Huck, as for Twain, many of the rules of civilization are confusing. Huck cannot understand why the Widow Douglas will not let him smoke when she herself takes snuff. But he knows a hypocrite when he sees one: "Of course that [taking snuff] was all right, because she done it herself."[65] These peccadilloes of the so-called civilized become major societal flaws when the issue is human rights. With this questioning of society's rules in an early chapter, Twain foreshadows the novel's major issue: slavery. A society in which men subject others to a life of servitude is not a civilized one, Twain suggests.

In the natural world, there is a sanctity that civilized life can never achieve. Nature is equated with freedom—for Huck and for Jim. Here men live as equals. Huck loves the wild so much that he is even willing to tolerate child abuse by his drunken ne'er-do-well father, Pap, to escape the strictures of Miss Watson and the Widow Douglas. After each sordid adventure on shore, Huck and Jim return to the relative quiet of life on the raft, where they are naked to the sun and the moon, the wind and the rain. Life on the river is natural. "It's lovely to live on a raft,"[66] Huck says.

Huck's decision to "light out for the territory" at the end of the novel is an attempt to recapture the freedom that he felt so briefly on his trip downriver, a freedom interrupted by the king and the duke, Jim's capture, and all that followed. But Twain knows better than Huck. In the 1830s, when the novel takes place, the Indian territory is ripe for exploring. But by the 1880s, when Twain published his novel, the territory had been largely overrun by "the rest" that Huck so ardently wished to avoid. Twain suggests that the freedom and naturalness Huck craves is only temporary, that "sivilization" is always on his heels.

Growing Up

Huck Finn is a book about a boy growing up, and his flight down the Mississippi River symbolizes his development. Not only is the Mississippi the prime mover of the novel's action, but it also serves as a metaphor for life itself, with all of its glory and dangers. The road to adulthood is never an easy one, particularly for a young boy faced with such weighty problems as is Huck. Though the river often functions as a place of escape, it is by no means completely safe. Just as the road of life has its bumps, so the Mississippi is fraught with danger. There are murderers on the river, and Jim and Huck are separated in the fog and placed at the mercy of a sadistic steamboat captain who purposely steers through their raft.

Huck's development as a person is also gauged by his response to Jim's humanity. As biographer Everett Emerson writes, two episodes in particular highlight Huck's growth. Both begin

> with Huck playing practical jokes on Jim. After the first badly misfires, Huck guiltily hides the evidence that

An artist's rendering of boat traffic on the Mississippi. In Twain's story, the great river symbolizes life itself and, more particularly, Huck's journey down the river symbolizes his moral development.

would show Jim to have been bitten by a rattlesnake as a result of "some fun" Huck has attempted. In the second, Huck makes a dramatic apology for the trick he has played on Jim in having pretended that their separation in the fog was only something Jim has dreamed.[67]

Huck's decision to take responsibility for his actions following the second practical joke is a measure of both his personal growth and his recognition of Jim's humanity. In apologizing to Jim, he violates a taboo in southern society by acknowledging Jim's worth: "It was fifteen minutes before I could work myself up to go and humble myself to a nigger—but I done it, and I warn't ever sorry for it afterwards, neither. I didn't do him no more mean tricks, and I wouldn't done that one if I'd a knowed it would make him feel that way."[68]

Huck grows morally, physically, and emotionally as he sails from Missouri to Louisiana with his friend and father figure, Jim. The reader watches as he comes of age, moving from the innocence of childhood to the responsibility of adulthood. He learns to make decisions for himself, to protect other people, and to do what his heart tells him is the right thing.

Heart Versus Mind

Huck's continual debate over whether or not to turn in Jim as an escaped slave takes the form of a battle between his "sound heart" and "deformed conscience." Society has conditioned Huck's mind to believe that slavery is acceptable. He worries that if he helps Jim to escape, "people would call me a low-down Ablitionist and despise me for keeping mum."[69] Nevertheless he continues in his quest to free Jim—in his heart he knows the value of Jim's loyalty and friendship and that something is wrong with a civilization that enslaves such a man.

But remaining loyal to Jim does not come easy for Huck. He continually has pangs of guilt, as when he hears Jim say that he will free his children after securing his own freedom:

> Thinks I, this is what comes of my not thinking. Here was this nigger which I had as good as helped to run away, coming right out flat-footed and saying he would steal his children—children that belonged to a man I didn't even know; a man that hadn't ever done me no harm.[70]

The climax of Huck's debate between mind and heart comes when he writes the letter to Miss Watson after Jim has been betrayed back into captivity by the loathesome king. When Huck tears up the letter and resolves to steal Jim from the Phelps plantation, he believes that he will be eternally damned for doing so—"All right, then, I'll *go* to hell,"[71] he tells himself. But Huck's friendship with Jim overshadows all of his fears of otherworldly retribution for his supposed sins. And the reader admires Huck's bravery in doing the right thing.

The Dark Side of Mankind

"Human beings *can* be awful cruel to one another,"[72] Huck asserts upon seeing the horrific sight of his former companions the king and duke tarred and feathered and ridden out of town on a rail by a mob of townspeople. The novel is filled with scenes of cruelty and barbarism, casting a dim light on American civilization. In *The Adventures of Huckleberry Finn*, Twain shows that he is well on the way to becoming the pessimistic writer who would later disparage humanity as "that damned human race."

As Huck sails downriver, he encounters the following horrific events: the search for escaped slaves by bounty hunters; the Shepherdson–Grangerford feud; Colonel Sherburn's murder of the harmless drunk Boggs; the king and duke's progressively more harmful scams; and the final tarring and feathering of the two con men.

Throughout his career, Mark Twain wrote against human cruelty wherever he saw it, hoping that readers might recognize their own flaws and reform themselves. Twain didn't necessarily believe such conversions were possible—witness the judge's failed attempt to reform Pap Finn early in the novel—but he felt the need to speak out and uphold righteousness and humane treatment of others whenever he could.

The Evils of Slavery and Racism

By making Jim a hero in *The Adventures of Huckleberry Finn* and through Huck's complex internal debate over freeing Jim, Twain provides a highly realistic picture of the complications inherent in the slave system and a vehement condemnation of that system. But Twain would never write a didactic moral treatise. He could not merely write a book stating that slavery was bad and that anyone who believed in it was evil. After all, he had grown up in a slaveholding state, where many morally upright people owned slaves. In Huck's internal struggle, though, Twain created a microcosm of the debate over slavery in America.

Contrasting *The Adventures of Huckleberry Finn* with *Uncle Tom's Cabin*, the other most frequently noted nineteenth-century novel about slavery, readers see a marked difference. Harriet Beecher Stowe wrote *Uncle Tom's Cabin* while slavery was still in place, and so the book functions as an anti-slavery polemic. It is a powerful, disturbing book but also a melodramatic one, with characters who are either purely good or evil. It has a simple message: Slavery is an evil institution that corrupts all it touches. *The Adventures of Huckleberry Finn*, written after the end of slavery but while African Americans were still treated as second-class citizens—or worse—is more subtle in its message. Jim is used, tricked, painted up, captured, beaten, and abused. Such abuse is symbolic of the treatment blacks received during the Reconstruction period (1865–77) following the Civil War. Many slaves, freed from the plantation or other service, now faced increased hardships. Most southern whites, still bitter over the Civil War, objected strongly to citizenship for former slaves, leading to the formation of hate organizations such as the Ku Klux Klan. The Klan's violent actions kept many African Americans living in fear and prevented their full incorporation into American life.

Such abuse takes on deeper meanings when the reader considers that Jim is a free man for much of the novel—Miss Watson had set him free in her will well before the novel's conclusion. This plot twist leads to speculation that Twain's real target was not slavery but its aftermath. When Twain wrote *The Adventures of Huckleberry Finn*, slavery was a dead institution, but African Americans—like the freed slave Jim—were still subject to racism and terrible treatment at the hands of whites.

Appearance Versus Reality

In *The Adventures of Huckleberry Finn,* as in life, what one sees and the reality behind visual perception are not always the same thing. Appearances can be deceiving. Again and again, Twain suggests that one has to see beyond the superficial in order to recognize the truth. In order for Huck to grow as a character, he must learn to see through such deception. Such is the case with his initial perception of slavery as an acceptable institution in southern society and his later realization that African Americans have the same hopes and dreams, and deserve the same rights, as their white counterparts.

In chapter 22, when Huck visits the circus, Twain provides a pointed example of how easy it is to be fooled by appearances. Huck enjoys the acts but feels sorry for a drunk man who enters the ring wanting to ride a horse. After much confusion, the ringleader allows the man to ride, and, at first, he makes a complete fool of himself, almost falling off the horse. But by the end of the act, Huck realizes that the man is actually a circus performer who rides faster and faster, performing daredevil tricks while moving at top speed.

Huck, and the reader along with him, have been duped. *The Adventures of Huckleberry Finn* is full of such confidence men, of characters who act one way and turn out to be something more sinister. The Grangerfords and Shepherdsons, Colonel Sherburn, the king and duke, even Huck himself, continually confuse other characters and the reader with their actions. In Twain's novel the pre–Civil War South is a dangerous place for the gullible.

Consequently, those who cannot disguise their appearance, especially the honest, sincere, and good-hearted, often fall prey to those who can. When Huck divulges the king and duke's scheme to Mary Jane Wilks, he knows that she can no longer stay in town because she will not be able to conceal her knowledge long enough for Huck to enact his scheme to right the con men's wrongs. As Huck explains to Mary Jane, she is not "one of those leather-face people." " I don't want no better book than what your face is," he adds. "A body can set down and read it off like coarse print."[73] Mary Jane's sincerity may be admirable, but not in this situation. As John C. Bird writes, "In contrast to Mary Jane, Huck is one of those leather-face people, and judging from the number of times he lies successfully, he is one of the most leather-face people who ever lived."[74]

"Honor bright now—no lies,"[75] the king says to Huck when he wants to know who has stolen the gold. "Honor bright," Huck repeats, then proceeds to lie. There is no honor among thieves, and Huck, by necessity, has become one of them. He is a character of many disguises—Sarah Williams, George Jackson, Adolphus, and Tom Sawyer among them—as he himself creates appearances that are not real in order to function in a world that is full of duplicity. As many critics have argued, Huck's lying is an immoral means toward a moral end—helping Jim—but lying is so ingrained in Huck's character that many readers, especially nineteenth-century readers, have found him distasteful.

But Huck is only using the system against itself. As a character near the bottom of the social scale, he cannot hope to change society. On his own small level, however, he is able to attack the wrongs of civilization through his support of one of society's oppressed, Jim. Huck must continually deceive those who wish to do harm to himself and to Jim in order to survive and to further their quest. As opposed to those evil con men who are only out to make money, Huck is a benevolent con man who attempts to help others.

Technique in *The Adventures of Huckleberry Finn*

In order to highlight his themes and create a rich portrait of pre–Civil War America, Twain uses a number of sophisticated techniques. Among these are his use of the first-person narrator, his adaptation of two classic literary forms—the epic and the picaresque—and his use of satire to condemn those events and institutions that he finds distasteful in American culture.

First-Person Narrative

As in other great American first-person narratives such as *Moby Dick*, *The Great Gatsby*, and *The Catcher in the Rye*, in *The Adventures of Huckleberry Finn*, Mark Twain makes masterful use of point of view. Through the use of a first-person narrator such as Huck Finn, a skilled writer such as Twain can manipulate narrative, tone, and style to create a multileveled, textured work of art. In this novel, what Huck says and what Twain means are often two different things. The naive Huckleberry Finn sees the world through very different eyes than the mature Mark Twain. Thus Twain uses Huck's unsophisticated, untainted worldview to create comedy, satirize human behavior, and make serious comments on the nature of the world.

An example of how Twain creates comedy through Huck's naïveté occurs as Huck describes his schooling. "I had been to school," Huck tells the reader at the beginning of chapter 4, "and could spell, and read, and write just a little, and could say the multiplication table up to six times seven is thirty-five, and I don't reckon I could ever get any further if I was to live forever."[76] Of course, Twain and the reader know that six times seven is not thirty-five. In addition to providing sheer comedy, the passage sets up a contrast between Huck's limited book learning and his advanced street-smarts.

Later Twain has fun satirizing people's tendency to gloss over unpleasant concepts with nice words, called euphemisms:

> Mornings, before daylight, I slipped into corn fields and borrowed a watermelon, or a mushmelon, or a punkin, or some new corn, or things of that kind. Pap always said it warn't no harm to borrow things, if you meant to give them back, sometime; but the widow said it warn't anything but a soft name for stealing.[77]

Pap and the Widow Douglas (center) provide Huck with widely divergent views on morality.

"Borrowing" is Huck's euphemism for stealing, and the Widow Douglas knows better. After all, how can one give back a watermelon or pumpkin after it has been eaten?

Elsewhere, Huck's naïveté allows Twain to comment on the nature of art. In the Grangerford–Shepherdson chapters, Huck, whose knowledge of culture and art is elementary at best, examines the writings of Emmeline Grangerford. After reading Emmeline's thoroughly maudlin effort "Ode to Stephen Dowling Bots, Dec'd," Huck comments:

> If Emmeline Grangerford could make poetry like that before she was fourteen, there ain't no telling what she could a done by-and-by. Buck said she could rattle off

poetry like nothing. She didn't even have to stop to think.[78]

Huck is sincere, but Twain is having a good time satirizing the notion of culture in middle America. As any serious reader knows, poetry demands writers who think deeply, not those who don't even stop to think. Moreover, Emmeline's supposedly poignant tale of a little boy who falls down a well is hardly sophisticated verse. With its cheap rhymes (sicken-thicken), comic lines ("They got him out and emptied him"), and romanticized language ("His spirit was gone for to sport aloft / In the realms of the good and great"),[79] "Ode to Stephen Dowling Bots, Dec'd," is Twain's parody of serious poetry. That Huck cannot recogize its low caliber adds to his charm, but also allows Twain to work his satirical magic.

The Forms of *The Adventures of Huckleberry Finn*

The Adventures of Huckleberry Finn contains elements of two classic literary structures, the epic and the picaresque. As an epic tale, the great American novel *The Adventures of Huckleberry Finn* sums up the culture of an emerging civilization. In this regard, it may be compared to the great epics of civilization: Homer's *The Iliad* and *The Odyssey* (Greece), Virgil's *The Aeneid* (Rome), *Beowulf*, and Milton's *Paradise Lost* (England), *The Song of Roland* (France), and *El Cid* (Spain).

Though Twain wrote the book in the late 1870s and early 1880s, the 1830s America he writes of was only fifty years old. It was a new country, a fresh country, a land full of opportunity that offered the immigrant a fresh start. Though numerous early American writers had attempted to write an epic that would celebrate this fledgling culture, at the time Twain wrote *The Adventures of Huckleberry Finn* the definitive literary portrait of American life had yet to be penned.

Like many of the great epics of old, *The Adventures of Huckleberry Finn* combines a hero representative of his culture, a large cast of characters, a long journey or quest, a comradeship between two great friends, some fierce battles, and a triumphant ending.

The second literary form on which *The Adventures of Huckleberry Finn* is based, the picaresque narrative, developed in sixteenth-century Spain. The first such example was the anonymous narrative *Lazarillo de Tormes* (1554), the tale of a poor boy who makes his way in the world through deceit. But the model for Twain's novel was *The Adventures of Gil Blas of Santillane* (1715–35), by the French writer Alain-René Lesage. Lesage's tale concerns a young man who travels through Spain having many adventures. Whereas Twain uses the Mississippi River as a conduit for Huck's adventures, Lesage opted for the open road. After finishing *Tom Sawyer*, a novel told from the third-person point of view, Twain wrote to William Dean Howells on July 5, 1875, saying that he didn't "take the chap [Tom] beyond boyhood" because "I believe it would be fatal to do it in any shape but autobiographically— like *Gil Blas*."[80] Thus Twain's use of the first person in *The Adventures of Huck Finn* allows Huck to comment on the various characters he meets on his journey, just as Lesage's *Gil Blas* voices his observations of French society. *Gil Blas* was an influence on *Huck Finn* in still other ways. Notable for its realism and attention to detail, Lesage's novel was a forerunner of realistic novels such as Twain's.

The picaresque novel is a witty, satirical form that revolves around the exploits of a lower-class hero of dubious morals, often called a "rogue hero." This hero lives by his wits as he moves through the various strata of his society, from the poorest class to the most wealthy. The hero is constantly in and out of trouble but often uses his street-smarts to emerge from compromising situations. Twain's novel conforms very well to this model. The picaresque form allows Twain to comment on all segments of life in American antebellum society and, by extension, in post–Civil War society as well. Huck's journey through the heart of America is simultaneously a journey through its social classes.

The picaresque novel is also episodic. Various scenes may have little to do with one another, and entire scenes may be removed without markedly altering the plot as a whole. In *The Adventures of Huckleberry Finn,* various episodes give the novel texture, but few readers would disagree with the notion that the basic plot would stay the same if the Shepherdson–Grangerford chapters, or the Sherburn-Boggs sequence, or the Wilks affair were removed. In fact, most editions of the novel completely leave out the so-called "raftsman's passage," a long description of life on a large raft floating on the Mississippi that was originally part of chapter 16.

Satire

No discussion of *The Adventures of Huckleberry Finn* would be complete without making reference to its satiric nature. M. H. Abrams defines satire as

> the literary art of diminishing or derogating a subject by making it ridiculous and evoking toward it attitudes of amusement, contempt, scorn or indignation. It differs from the comic in that comedy evokes laughter mainly as an end in itself, while satire derides; that is, it uses laughter as a weapon.[81]

Like the great satirical writers Rabelais, Voltaire, Jonathan Swift, Joseph Heller, and Kurt Vonnegut, Twain is constantly poking fun at society. Sometimes the satire is rather lighthearted, as when Twain gently mocks the pretentious verse of Emmeline Grangerford, and, more to the point, writers and readers who consider such scribblings "poetry." Other times, Twain writes with what he would later call "a pen warmed up in Hell." The vicious chapters in which Colonel Sherburn shoots the harmless Boggs, then proceeds to deride his would-be lynch mob as a bunch of cowards, qualifies as an example of the latter, as Twain viciously satirizes life in backwoods small-town America and so-called "civilized" men who are driven to barbaric acts at the slightest provocation.

Satire, at its most sophisticated, can be very subtle—so subtle, that if readers fail to see the point, they may be highly offended. Some, but not all, of *The Adventures of Huckleberry Finn*'s troubles over the years derive from this quality of the satiric genre. An example is when Huck informs Aunt Sally that no one was injured in his invented steamboat accident even though he mentions that a black man was killed. Coupled with Sally's equally racially blind reply, "Well, it's lucky; because sometimes people do get hurt," [82] readers who fail to see that Twain is satirizing racist thinking that does not grant humanity to African Americans may indeed want to label the novel "racist trash."

Though slavery is the main evil in *The Adventures of Huckleberry Finn*, a satiric reading of the novel suggests that Twain's attack on slavery is only a means toward an end. For Twain to have published a novel in the 1880s that satirized slavery, a dead institution, would have limited its effectiveness. Therefore, as some contemporary critics (Victor Doyno, for example) have suggested, Twain's true target is the racism and abuse of African Americans that continued almost unabated in America long after the Civil War.

Notes

Introduction: What a Trouble It Was

1. Ernest Hemingway, *The Green Hills of Africa*. New York: Scribner's, 1963, p. 22.

2. Clifton Fadiman, *Huckleberry Finn: Three Filmed Lessons in the Humanities*. Encyclopedia Britannica Films, 1965.

3. Mark Twain, *The Adventures of Huckleberry Finn*. Berkeley: University of California Press, 1985, p. 362.

4. Twain, *Huckleberry Finn*, p. 166.

5. Asa Don Dickinson, "Huckleberry Finn is Fifty Years Old—Yes; But is He Respectable?" *Wilson Bulletin for Librarians*, 10, November 1935, p. 183.

Chapter 1: Biography of Samuel Langhorne Clemens

6. Luke Pease, "Mark Twain Talks," *Portland Oregonian*, August 11, 1895.

7. Andrew Hoffman, *Inventing Mark Twain: The Lives of Samuel Langhorne Clemens*. New York: William Morrow, 1997, pp. 9–10.

8. Mark Twain, *The Adventures of Tom Sawyer*. Berkeley: University of California Press, 1984, p. 47.

9. Mark Twain, *The Autobiography of Mark Twain*. New York: Harper & Row, 1959, p. 32.

10. Twain, *Autobiography*, p. 87.

11. Dixon Wechter, *Sam Clemens of Hannibal*. Boston: Houghton Mifflin, 1952, pp. 65, 264.

12. Hoffman, *Inventing Mark Twain*, p. 45.

13. John Lauber, *The Making of Mark Twain: A Biography*. New York: American Heritage, 1985, p. 115.

14. Mark Twain, *Roughing It*. Berkeley: University of California Press, 1983, p. 376.

15. Bernard DeVoto, *Mark Twain's America*. Lincoln: University of Nebraska Press, 1997, p. 166.

16. Twain, *Autobiography*, p. 174.

17. Robert Keith Miller, *Mark Twain*. New York: Frederick Ungar, 1983, p. 19.

18. Henry Nash Smith and William M. Gibson, eds., *Mark Twain–Howells Letters*, vol. 1. Cambridge: Harvard University Press, 1960, p. 144.

19. Twain, *Autobiography*, p. 264.

20. Walter Blair, *Mark Twain and Huck Finn*. Berkeley: University of California Press, 1960, p. 2.

21. Quoted in Albert Bigelow Paine, *Mark Twain: A Biography*, vol. II. New York: Harper & Brothers, 1912, p. 1039.

22. Justin Kaplan, *Mr. Clemens and Mark Twain: A Biography*. New York: Simon & Schuster, 1966, p. 339.

23. Kaplan, *Mr. Clemens and Mark Twain*, p. 380.

24. William Dean Howells, *My Mark Twain*. New York: Harper & Brothers, 1910, p. 101.

Chapter 2: Historical Background

25. Mark Twain, "Fenimore Cooper's Literary Offenses," in *Great Short Works of Mark Twain*, ed. Justin Kaplan. New York: Harper & Row, 1967, p. 170.

26. Richard Lederer, *The Miracle of Language*. New York: Pocket, 1991, p. 125.

27. Twain, *Huckleberry Finn*, p. 1.

28. Twain, *Autobiography*, p. 3.

29. Twain, *Autobiography*, p. 6.

30. Twain, *Autobiography*, p. 2.

31. Twain, *Autobiography*, pp. 5–6.

32. Twain, *Autobiography*, p. 6.

33. Twain, *Autobiography*, p. 68.

34. Hoffman, *Inventing Mark Twain*, p. 18.

35. Quoted in Blair, *Mark Twain and Huck Finn*, p. 143.

36. Quoted in Blair, *Mark Twain and Huck Finn*, p. 144.

37. Twain, *Autobiography*, p. 68.

38. Lauber, *The Making of Mark Twain*, p. 142.

39. Lauber, *The Making of Mark Twain*, p. 26.

40. Resa Willis, *Mark and Livy: The Love Story of Mark Twain and the Woman Who Almost Tamed Him.* New York: Atheneum, 1992, p. 16.

41. Twain, *Huckleberry Finn*, p. 52.

42. Quoted in Edwin McDowell, "From Twain, a Letter on Debt to Blacks," *New York Times*, March 14, 1985, sec. I, p. 1.

43. Quoted in McDowell, "From Twain, a Letter on Debt to Blacks," sec. III, p. 21.

44. *New York Herald*, March 18, 1855.

45. John H. Wallace, "*Huckleberry Finn* Is Racist Trash," *Chicago Sun-Times*. May 25, 1984, p. A23.

46. Nicholas J. Karolides, Margaret Bald, and Dawn B. Sova, *100 Banned Books: Censorship Histories of World Literature.* New York: Checkmark, 1999, p. 337.

47. "Born to Trouble: *Adventures of Huckleberry Finn*," www.pbs.org/wgbh/cultureshock/beyond/huck.html.

Chapter 3: The Plot

48. Twain, *Huckleberry Finn*, pp. 20, 22.

49. Twain, *Huckleberry Finn*, pp. 23, 36.

50. Twain, *Huckleberry Finn*, p. 52.

51. Twain, *Huckleberry Finn*, p. 75.

52. Twain, *Huckleberry Finn*, p. 142.

53. Twain, *Huckleberry Finn*, p. 271.

54. Twain, *Huckleberry Finn*, p. 297.

55. Twain, *Huckleberry Finn*, p. 362.

Chapter 4: The Cast of Characters

56. Twain, *Huckleberry Finn*, p. 279.

57. Bernard W. Bell, "Twain's 'Nigger' Jim: The Tragic Face Behind the Minstrel Mask," in *Satire or Evasion? Black Perspectives on Huckleberry Finn*, eds. James S. Leonard, Thomas A. Tenney, and Thadious M. Davis. Durham, NC: Duke University Press, 1992, p. 138.

58. Twain, *Huckleberry Finn*, p. 160.

59. Twain, *Huckleberry Finn*, p. 144.

Chapter Five: Literary Analysis

60. Twain, *Huckleberry Finn*, p. 142.

61. Twain, *Huckleberry Finn*, p. 199.

62. Twain, *Huckleberry Finn*, p. 200.

63. Shelley Fisher Fishkin, *Lighting Out for the Territory: Reflections on Mark Twain and American Culture*. New York: Oxford University Press, 1997, p. 6.

64. Twain, *Huckleberry Finn*, pp. 1, 3.

65. Twain, *Huckleberry Finn*, p. 3.

66. Twain, *Huckleberry Finn*, p. 158.

67. Everett Emerson, *Mark Twain: A Literary Life*. Philadelphia: University of Pennsylvania Press, 2000, p. 145.

68. Twain, *Huckleberry Finn*, p. 105.

69. Twain, *Huckleberry Finn*, pp. 52–53.

70. Twain, *Huckleberry Finn*, p. 124.

71. Twain, *Huckleberry Finn*, p. 271.

72. Twain, *Huckleberry Finn*, p. 290.

73. Twain, *Huckleberry Finn*, p. 242.

74. John C. Bird, "'These Leather-Face People': Huck and the Moral Act of Lying," *Studies in American Fiction*, 15, no. 1, spring 1987, p. 71.

75. Twain, *Huckleberry Finn*, p. 235.

76. Twain, *Huckleberry Finn*, p. 18.

77. Twain, *Huckleberry Finn*, pp. 79–80.

78. Twain, *Huckleberry Finn*, p. 140.

79. Twain, *Huckleberry Finn*, p. 139.

80. Quoted in Smith and Gibson, *Mark Twain–Howells Letters*, p. 91.

81. M. H. Abrams, *A Glossary of Literary Terms*, 7th ed. Fort Worth, TX: Harcourt Brace, 1999, p. 275.

82. Twain, *Huckleberry Finn*, p. 279.

For Further Exploration

Below are some suggestions for potential essays on *The Adventures of Huckleberry Finn*.

1. During the course of the novel, Huck engages in a continual debate between his conscience, which tells him that helping Jim is a sin, and his heart, which acknowledges Jim's humanity and his right to be a free man. Trace this debate through the novel and ascertain whether either side ultimately "wins" this debate. *See* Henry Nash Smith, *Mark Twain: The Development of a Writer*. Cambridge, MA: Belknap Press, 1962, pp. 113–37.

2. Leo Marx, a well-known critic of *The Adventures of Huckleberry Finn*, concludes, "The flimsy devices of plot, the discordant farcical [comical] tone, and the disintegration of the major characters all betray the failure of the ending." By giving examples, show how you agree or disagree with the three claims that Marx makes. Does the ending ruin or enhance the idea that *The Adventures of Huckleberry Finn* is a great novel? *See* Leo Marx, "Mr. Eliot, Mr. Trilling and Huckleberry Finn," in *The Pilot and the Passenger: Essays on Literature, Technology, and Culture in the United States*. New York: Oxford University Press, 1988; Lionel Trilling, "Introduction," *The Adventures of Huckleberry Finn*. New York: Holt, Rinehart and Winston, 1950. Reprinted in Lionel Trilling, *The Liberal Imagination: Essays in Literature and Society*. New York: Scribner's, 1950; T. S. Eliot, "Introduction," *The Adventures of Huckleberry Finn*. New York: Chanticleer Press, 1950.

3. The novelist Jane Smiley has argued that she would rather children read *Uncle Tom's Cabin*, another great antislavery novel, than *The Adventures of Huckleberry Finn*. Read and compare the two novels. Do you prefer one novel over the other? Why or why not? Consider the strengths and weaknesses of the books as you formulate your answer. *See* Harriet Beecher Stowe, *Uncle Tom's Cabin, or Life Among the Lowly*. New York: Penguin, 1981; Jane Smiley, "Say It Ain't So, Huck," *Harper's Magazine*, January 1996, pp. 61–67; Justin Kaplan, "Selling 'Huck Finn' Down the River," *New York Times*, March 10, 1996, p. 27.

4. Some critics have claimed that *Huckleberry Finn* is a racist book. What do you think? Cite specific examples from the text to support your argument. *See* John H. Wallace, "*Huckleberry Finn* Is Racist Trash," *Chicago Sun-Times*, May 25, 1984, p. A23; "Huck, Continued," *The New Yorker*, June 26–July 3, 1995, pp. 130–33; Thadious M. Davis, ed., "Black Writers on *Adventures*

of Huckleberry Finn: One Hundred Years Later," *Mark Twain Journal* 22, no. 2, fall 1984.

5. Investigate the history of runaway slaves in America. How realistic is Twain's depiction of Jim's escape in *Huckleberry Finn*? *See* Jocelyn Chadwick-Joshua, *The Jim Dilemma: Reading Race in Huckleberry Finn*. Jackson: University of Mississippi Press, 1998; Frederick Douglass, *Life and Times of Frederick Douglass*. New York: Macmillan, 1962; Henry Louis Gates Jr., ed., *The Classic Slave Narratives*. New York: Penguin, 1987.

6. In the summer of 1876, Twain stopped writing *Huckleberry Finn* for three years, pausing at the point where Huck and Jim dive off their raft as a steamboat comes barreling through. Why do you think Twain stopped at this point? What problems were there in the narrative that must have given him pause about how to proceed? Where is his frustration evident in the narrative? *See* Walter Blair, *Mark Twain and Huck Finn*. Berkeley: University of California Press, 1960.

7. While *The Adventures of Huckleberry Finn* is literally a book about slavery, Twain was writing in a time when slavery was no longer an issue. Given that Twain was a social satirist, how does his book reflect actual concerns about the poor treatment of African Americans in the post–Civil War era? *See* Victor Doyno, *Writing Huck Finn: Mark Twain's Creative Process*. Philadelphia: University of Pennsylvania Press, 1993; Peter Messent, *Mark Twain*. New York: St. Martin's Press, 1997, pp. 86–109.

8. Huck continually lies during the novel, telling falsehoods to everyone from Tom's Aunt Sally and Uncle Silas to the king and duke. Are his lies defensible or is he merely a liar? Give examples to support your claim. *See* Gladys C. Bellamy, *Mark Twain as a Literary Artist*. Norman: University of Oklahoma Press, 1950, pp. 336–37; Henry Nash Smith, "Introduction," *The Adventures of Huckleberry Finn*. Boston: Houghton Mifflin, 1958.

9. *The Adventures of Huckleberry Finn* continually contrasts life on the Mississippi River with life along the shore. How does Twain use these settings to comment on nineteenth-century America? *See* Lionel Trilling, "Introduction," *The Adventures of Huckleberry Finn*. New York: Holt, Rinehart and Winston, 1950; T. S. Eliot, "Introduction," *The Adventures of Huckleberry Finn*. New York: Chanticleer Press, 1950.

10. Given that many critics believe the ending of *Huckleberry Finn* is the weakest part of the novel, how would you end the novel if you could rewrite it? Explain and defend your decisions. *See*

James M. Cox, *Mark Twain: The Fate of Humor*. Princeton: Princeton University Press, 1966, pp. 172–84; Leo Marx, "Mr. Eliot, Mr. Trilling and Huckleberry Finn," in *The Pilot and the Passenger: Essays on Literature, Technology, and Culture in the United States*. New York: Oxford University Press, 1988; John Seelye, *The True Adventures of Huckleberry Finn*. Evanston, IL: Northwestern University Press, 1970.

Appendix of Criticism

The Adventures of Huckleberry Finn Is a Wearisome Book

Mark Twain's *The Adventures of Huckleberry Finn* had a certain relishable flavor when mixed up with the miscellaneous assortment of magazine literature; but in a book form, and covering more than 350 pages, they are wearisome and labored. It would be about as easy to read through a jest book, as to keep up one's interest in the monotonous humor and the dialectic variations of *Huck Finn*'s narrative. Here and there are spatches of Mark Twain's best work, which could be read over and over again, and yet bring each time an outburst of laugher; but one cannot have the book long in his hands without being tempted to regret that the author should so often have laid himself open to the charge of coarseness and bad taste. The illustrations are admirable in their way. As to the general character of the book, it may be sufficient to remind the reader of the author's notice, that "all persons attempting to find a motive in this narrative will be prosecuted; persons attempting to find a moral in it will be banished; persons attempting to find a plot in it will be shot."

Boston Daily Advertiser, March 12, 1885, p. 2.

Too Much Fanfare, Too Little Story

Mark Twain long since learned the art of writing for the market. His recent books have the character of commercial ventures. He probably estimates in advance his profits. His books are not sold to any great extent over the counters of booksellers, but are circulated by subscription agents. Lately Mark Twain, it is reported, has become the silent partner in a publishing house, the imprint of which is on the present volume. Those who read *Tom Sawyer* and like it will probably read *Huckleberry Finn*, and like it in a less degree. No book has been put on the market with more advertising. When Mark Twain represented *Tom Sawyer* as getting a job of free white-washing done by his cronies, because there was fun in it, and only just enough to go around, he disclosed his own tactics in the matter of free advertising. When it was given out that some one had tampered with the engravings in the printing office, in a mysterious way, that accounted for the delay in bringing out the book, it secured at the same time many thousand dollars' worth of free advertising. Then the *Century* [magazine] gave the enterprise a lift by publishing a chapter of the book in advance, which, while an advertisement, was still a readable article. *Huckleberry Finn* has been introduced to the world as it were with the blare of trumpets. It comes also with this warning: "Persons attempting to find a motive in this narrative will be prosecuted; persons attempting to find a moral in it will be banished; persons attempting to find a plot in it will be shot." So then there is neither motive, moral, nor plot. . . .

The author starts out by telling his juvenile readers that there are some lies in his book—that most people lie, and that it is not very bad after all. Of course the warning is timely that persons attempting to seek a moral in the story should be banished. . . .

It is an amusing story if such scrap-work can be called a story. The author rarely fails when he sets out to tickle the ribs of young or old. There is so little genuine wit in the world, that the little must be made to go a great way. Mark Twain has the genuine vein; it nearly pinches out here and there, and in many places it is hardly an inch wide by miners' measurement. The funny book will always be read in this world of dryness and dearth. Many fastidious people hide their scruples, because they want to be amused. Comedy pays better than tragedy. The author contrives to puncture a great many shams. His satire in this respect, even when he declares that it is aimless, is directed with a purpose. Whether young people who read this volume will be the better for it will be an open question.

San Francisco Evening Bulletin, March 14, 1885, p. 1.

The Adventures of Huckleberry Finn Is More Grotesque than Funny

Mark Twain is a humorist or nothing. He is well aware of the fact himself, for he prefaces the *Adventures of Huckleberry Finn* with a brief notice, warning persons in search of a moral, motive or plot that they are liable to be prosecuted, banished or shot. This is a nice little artifice to scare off the critics—a kind of "trespassers on these grounds will be dealt with according to law."

However, as there is no penalty attached, we organized a search expedition for the humorous qualities of this book with the following hilarious results:

A very refined and delicate piece of narration by Huck Finn, describing his venerable and dilapidated "pap" as afflicted with delirium tremens, rolling over and over, "kicking things every which way," and "saying there are devils ahold of him." This chapter is especially suited to amuse the children on long, rainy afternoons.

An elevating and laughable description of how Huck killed a pig, smeared its blood on an axe and mixed in a little of his own hair, and then ran off, setting up a job on the old man and the community, and leading them to believe him murdered. This little joke can be repeated by any smart boy for the amusement of his fond parents.

A graphic and romantic tale of a Southern family feud, which resulted in an elopement and from six to eight choice corpses.

A polite version of the "Giascutus" story, in which a nude man, striped with the colors of the rainbow, is exhibited as "The King's Camelopard; or, The Royal Nonesuch." This is a chapter for lenten parlor entertainments and church festivals.

A side-splitting account of a funeral, enlivened by a "sick melodeun," a "long-legged undertaker," and rat episode in the cellar.

Life, February 26, 1885, p. 119.

Young Twain and the Ethics of Slavery

In 1846, when Sam Clemens was old enough to begin to think about moral distinctions, the Dred Scott case began in Missouri. This case centered on three issues: Was a slave who had been brought by his master to live in a non-slave territory free? Was a child the slave fathered there free? Could the father be reenslaved by being returned to Missouri? The case commanded much attention because it so clearly illustrated the terrible conflict between human or familial rights and property rights. For eleven years, with extensive news coverage, the case was tried, decided, and appealed in Missouri and in the federal courts. Dred Scott and his child were ultimately declared mere chattels, slaves who could be moved anywhere. The Supreme Court additionally advised that the limits on slavery in the Missouri Compromise were illegal and that Congress could make no laws restricting slavery. Slavery was in an expansionist mode.

Another law proved equally or even more controversial. Sam was fifteen when the Second Fugitive Slave Act (1850) showed how the issue of slavery could destroy any national consensus. Under this law, federal marshals were ordered to help slave catchers. Interference was illegal. Part of the law specifed that a person accused of being an escaped slave could not call any witnesses to help establish his or her history. The presiding magistrate or judge would get five dollars if he found the accused to be a free person, and ten dollars if he decided that the accused was a slave. (The modern equivalent of ten dollars would be well over a hundred dollars.) Angry feelings ran high; the state of Wisconsin threatened to secede from the Union.

During these turbulent times, when Sam Clemens' values were crystallizing, central moral issues were being debated: individual decisionmaking, political obedience, nullification (the right of an individual or a state to disobey any law it disagreed with), the abolition of slavery, and the role of custom and religion in shaping personal choices. How complex, confusing, baffling all these problems must have seemed to a highly intelligent boy who had been forced by family poverty to drop out of school at age twelve, after his father's death, and take up newspaper work. As an adolescent "jour printer" Sam educated himself while setting acres of type, including local, regional, and national news, and many articles and essays that were simply reprinted from other newspapers.

Thus, when Mark Twain's fictional creation Huck Finn repeatedly debates with himself about his attempts to help Jim, the modern reader may read/listen/think with sympathy as a child tries to tell right from wrong and as an adult author imaginatively reconsiders his own youth, his own moral dilemmas, as well as his own and his country's ethical and political development.

Victor Doyno, "Afterword," *The Adventures of Huckleberry Finn.* New York: Oxford University Press, 1996, pp. 3–5.

Mississippi River Valley Violence Affected Young Samuel Clemens

The Adventures of Huckleberry Finn has so much about it that is hilarious or idyllic that our attention is easily diverted from the spill of blood that seeps through its pages, giving them a large part of their meaning. Life on the Mississippi around 1845 could be gory: Twain based the novel largely on experiences he himself had undergone as a boy or had known intimately of, and had never quite got over. We are often disinclined to consider how peaceful and restricted, aside from television, is the average recent American childhood compared to childhoods of other times and of other places today. Many people have become adults without ever having seen "live" a human being killed. Plenty of boys have never looked at a corpse, and very few of them have witnessed a murder.

Things were different with young Clemens and thus with Huck. The difference is profoundly important to the novel. Sam often looked hard at slaves chained together flat on the dirt in the baking summer sun, awaiting shipment to the market. He was a boy in Hannibal during a time when that town was terrorized by a lynching, murderous gang ludicrously called "The Black Avengers of the Spanish Main." A cave near Hannibal contained as a public amusement the body of a young girl preserved in alcohol; it was arranged so that one could seize the corpse by the hair, and drag it to the surface in order to study the face. When he was ten years old the boy saw a man take a lump of iron and crush a Negro's skull with it; then Sam spent an hour in fascinated horror watching the slave die. One night he heard a drunk announce that he was going to the house of a certain widow for the express purpose of raping her daughter, and Sam followed him, lurking close by while he bellowed his intentions outside the girl's house. The widow approached the man with defiance, counted ten, and then gave the swaying fellow a musket charge full in the chest. At this point the townspeople collected like ants, but Sam had had enough. He went home to dream of the murder and was not disappointed, he says.

One night it was not a dream. Trying to sleep in his father's office, he became aware of some awful presence, and shortly the moon revealed a naked corpse with a hole in the middle of its chest. On another occasion he was playing near the spot where a runaway slave had drowned days before, and by accident he jarred loose the body, which had not been located, but which now popped up at him headfirst half out of the water, and seemed certainly to be chasing him as he fled. He watched knife fights in

101

Hannibal, and at the end of one of them the loser fell dead at the feet of the boy who had wormed his way in for a good look. He was also witness, at noon on Main Street, to the murder of a man named Smarr. Kind persons placed a large Bible on the chest of the dying man. As he wrote years later, Sam "gasped and struggled for breath under the crush of that vast book for many a night."

The murders of Mr. Smarr and of the drunkard who was shot in the chest by the contemptuous widow are the direct sources for the murder of a man named Boggs in *Huckleberry Finn*. Of the shocks young Clemens was exposed to as a boy, many others found their way, years later, into the novel. These facts help explain what might otherwise seem a very curious thing: that with no exceptions but the rather irrelevant Tom Sawyer scenes which open and close *Huckleberry Finn*, every major episode in the novel ends in violence, in physical brutality, and usually in death. All along the way there is bloodshed and pain. There are thirteen separate corpses. All this despite the fact that Twain, in planning his book, made many notes for similar episodes which he did not use.

Phillip Young, *Three Bags Full: Essays in American Fiction*. New York: Harvest, 1967, pp. 147–49.

Huck Is Basically Kindhearted

Basically honest, Huck nonetheless tells lies throughout the novel, lies which are excusable only because they are absurdly transparent. When he masquerades as a girl and visits St. Petersburg in order to learn the local news, he does such a bad job of it that his disguise is quickly penetrated. He cannot even remember the name he has assumed, a tendency which afflicts him at the Grangerfords as well. After he has forgotten his assumed name, he has to trick Buck Grangerford into revealing it to him, and he then has to write it down so he won't forget it again. When he is interrogated by Joanna Wilks a few chapters later, he lies as cleverly as he can. Nonetheless, he is obliged to admit: "But I didn't do it pretty good, and when I got done I see she warn't satisfied." And when Aunt Sally plies him with questions upon his arrival at the Phelps plantation, he is clearly about to falter. He is not inventive enough to lie with the abandon of a Tom Sawyer, and he confesses, "I was getting so uneasy I couldn't listen good."

On at least one occasion, however, Huck lies very well indeed. He has been separated from Jim in a fog while scouting about in the canoe. Jim becomes convinced that Huck has drowned and bitterly mourns his loss. When Huck returns to the raft, Jim is asleep; he wakes him up and then pretends that he had never been off the raft: Jim must have dreamed the entire incident. Jim is momentarily taken in, but he eventually realizes that Huck is playing a cruel trick upon him. He rebukes Huck in an often cited scene:

> When I got all wore out wid work, en wid de callin' for you, en went to sleep, my heart wuz mos' broke bekase you wuz los', en I didn' k'yer no mo' what become er me en de raf'. En when I wake up en fine you back agin', all safe en soun', de tears come en I could a got down on my knees en kiss' yo' foot I's so thankful. En all you wuz thinkin 'bout wuz how you could make a fool uv ole Jim wid a lie. Dat truck dah is *trash;* en trash is what people is dat puts dirt on de head er dey fren's en makes 'em ashamed.

Huck is mortified, and he tells us, "I could almost kissed *his* foot to get him to take it back." He learns an important lesson: Jim is a man with feelings and not simply a runaway slave upon whom practical jokes can be played at random. "It was fifteen minutes before I could work myself up to go and humble myself to a nigger— but I done it, and I warn't ever sorry for it afterwards, neither. I didn't do him no more mean tricks, and I wouldn't done that one if I'd knowed it would make him feel that way." True to his word, Huck never lies to Jim again, although the stories he tells nearly everyone else reflect his belief that "a body that ups and tells the truth . . . is taking considerable many risks."

As this scene with Jim suggests, Huck is basically kindhearted. Despite a childhood positively drenched with violence, he is deeply troubled by the suffering of others. When he sees house lights burning late at night, he assumes that is "where there was sick folks, may be." When he steals a chicken for his supper, he takes care to choose one "that warn't roosting comfortable." And when he sees a circus performer delighting a crowd by pretending to fall off a horse, he records: "It warn't funny to me, though; I was all of a tremble to see his danger." More seriously, after witnessing the death of Buck Grangerford, he cannot tell us what he saw:

It made me so sick I most fell out of the tree. I ain't agoing to tell *all* that happened—it would make me sick again if I was to do that. I wished I hadn't ever come ashore that night, to see such things. I ain't ever going to get shut of them—lots of times I dream about them.

And he is also haunted by the memory of a slave auction, "the two sons [sold] up the river to Memphis, and their mother down the river to Orleans." Huck recounts, "I can't ever get it out of my memory, the sight of them poor miserable girls and niggers hanging around each other's necks and crying."

So great is Huck's capacity to sympathize with suffering that he even has pity for scoundrels. Early in the novel he worries about a gang of thieves trapped on a wrecked steamboat likely to sink at any moment: "I begun to think how dreadful it was, even for murderers, to be in such a fix. I says to myself, there ain't no telling but I might come to be a murderer myself, and then how would *I* like it?" And even after the king and the duke have engineered Jim's capture, Huck cannot bear to see them tarred and feathered:

Well it made me sick to see it; and I was sorry for them poor pitiful rascals, it seemed like I couldn't ever feel any hardness against them any more in the world. It was a dreadful thing to see. Human beings *can* be awful cruel to one another.

Robert Keith Miller, *Mark Twain*. New York: Frederick Ungar, 1983, pp. 93–95.

The Ending of *Huckleberry Finn* Is Unsatisfactory

I believe that the ending of *Huckleberry Finn* makes so many readers uneasy because they rightly sense that it jeopardizes the significance of the entire novel. To take seriously what happens at the Phelps farm is to take lightly the entire downstream journey. What is the meaning of the journey? With this question all discussion of *Huckleberry Finn* must begin. It is true that the voyage down the river has many aspects of a boy's idyl. We owe much of its hold upon our imagination to the enchanting image of the raft's unhurried drift with the current. The leisure, the absence of constraint, the beauty of the river—all these things delight us. "It's lovely to live on a raft." And the multitudinous life of the great valley we see through Huck's eyes has a fascination of its own. Then, of course, there is humor—laughter so spontaneous, so free of the bitterness present almost everywhere in American humor that readers often forget how grim a spectacle of human existence Huck contemplates. Humor in this novel flows from a bright joy of life as remote from our world as living on a raft.

Yet along with the idyllic and the epical and the funny in *Huckleberry Finn*, there is a coil of meaning which does for the disparate elements of the novel what a spring does for a watch. The meaning is not in the least obscure. It is made explicit again and again. The very words with which Clemens launches Huck and Jim upon their voyage indicate that theirs is not a boy's lark but a quest for freedom. From the electrifying moment when Huck comes back to Jackson's Island and rouses Jim with the news that a search party is on the way, we are meant to believe that Huck is enlisted in the cause of freedom. "Git up and hump yourself, Jim!" he cries. "There ain't a minute to lose. They're after us!" What particularly counts here is the *us*. No one is after Huck; no one but Jim knows he is alive. In that small word Clemens compresses the exhilarating power of Huck's instinctive humanity. His unpremeditated identification with Jim's flight from slavery is an unforgettable moment in American experience, and it may be said at once that any culmination of the journey which detracts from the urgency and dignity with which it begins will necessarily be unsatisfactory. Huck realizes this himself, and says so when, much later, he comes back to the raft after discovering that the Duke and the King have sold Jim:

> "After all this long journey . . . here it was all come to nothing, everything all busted up and ruined, because they could have the heart to serve Jim such a trick as that and make him a slave again all his life, and amongst strangers, too, for forty dirty dollars."

Huck knows that the journey will have been a failure unless it takes Jim to freedom. It is true that we do discover, in the end, that Jim is free, but we also find out that the journey was not the means by which he finally reached freedom.

The most obvious thing wrong with the end, then, is the flimsy contrivance by which Clemens frees Jim. In the end we discover not only that Jim has been a free man for two months, but that his freedom has been granted by old Miss Watson. If this were only a mechanical device for terminating the action, it might not call for much comment. But it is more than that: it is a significant clue to the import of the last ten chapters. Remember who Miss Watson is. She is the Widow's sister whom Huck introduces in the first pages of the novel. It is she who keeps "pecking" at Huck, who tries to teach him to spell and to pray and to keep his feet off the furniture. She is an ardent proselytizer for piety and good manners, and her greed provides the occasion for the journey in the first place. She is Jim's owner, and he decides to flee only when he realizes that she is about to break her word (she cannot resist a slave trader's offer of eight hundred dollars) and sell him down the river away from his family.

Miss Watson, in short, is the Enemy. If we except a predilection for physical violence, she exhibits all the outstanding traits of the valley society. She pronounces the polite lies of civilization that suffocate Huck's spirit. The freedom which Jim seeks, and which Huck and Jim temporarily enjoy aboard the raft, is accordingly freedom *from* everything for which Miss Watson stands. Indeed, the very intensity of the novel derives from the discordance between the aspirations of the fugitives and the respectable code for which she is a spokesperson. Therefore, her regeneration, of which the deathbed freeing of Jim is the unconvincing sign, hints a resolution of the novel's essential conflict. Perhaps because this device most transparently reveals that shift in point of view which he could not avoid, and which is less easily discerned elsewhere in the concluding chapters, Clemens plays it down. He makes little attempt to account for Miss Watson's change of heart, a change particularly surprising in view of Jim's brazen escape. Had Clemens given this episode a dramatic emphasis appropriate to its function, Miss Watson's bestowal of freedom upon Jim would have proclaimed what the rest of the ending actually accomplishes—a vindication of persons and attitudes Huck and Jim had symbolically repudiated when they set forth downstream.

Leo Marx, *The Pilot and the Passenger: Essays on Literature, Technology, and Culture in the United States.* New York: Oxford, 1988, pp. 39–41.

Twain Creates a New Language for the Novel

All other considerations aside, *Huckleberry Finn* would be an epoch-making book for this one reason alone—Twain's striking creation of literary Amerenglish. Above all it is the stress and flux of the novel's sentences, and the evocative power of its extraordinary vocabulary, which leaves the reader with his sense of having been along the river with Huck Finn. The tensile strength in the following passage, for example, which displays Twain's inventiveness at its best, derives as much from para-neologisms as "spider-webby" and "blue-black" as the build-up assault on our imaginative senses. Twain's prose here, in its cumulative intensity, is a microcosmic expression of his success in the novel as a whole:

> Directly it began to rain, and it rained like all fury, too, and I never see the wind blow so. It was one of these regular summer storms. It would get so dark that it looked all blue-black outside, and lovely; and the rain would thrash along by so thick that the trees off a little ways looked dim and spider-webby; and here would come a blast of wind that would bend the trees down and turn up the pale underside of the leaves; and then a perfect ripper of a gust would follow along and set the branches to tossing their arms as if they was just wild; and next, when it was just about the bluest and blackest—*fst!* it was as bright as glory and you'd have a little glimpse of tree-tops a-plunging about, away off yonder in the storm, hundreds of yards further than you could see before; dark as sin again in a second, and now you'd hear the thunder let go with an awful crash and then go rumbling, grumbling, tumbling down the sky towards the under side of the world, like rolling empty barrels down stairs, where it's long stairs and they bounce a good deal, you know.

This celebrated passage is so graphic that one realises with surprise that its decisive sentence, stylistically speaking, is also its most banal and prosaic: "It was one of these regular summer storms." The approach to what is typical and representative, in this case as elsewhere in the novel, is what releases Twain from the oppression of self-conscious poetry—Victorian prettiness—allowing him to indulge his descriptive powers to the full without appearing to strain for dramatic effect. Yet it is a highly theatrical, one might almost say Gothic, passage, full of vivid effects made up by the accumulation of a series of painterly details: the dark sky and driving rain, the pale undersides of the leaves flashing in the lightning, and the rolling thunder disappearing below the horizon. Twain creates an almost hypnotic mood in just a few sentences, and then snaps us out of it gently with Huck's disingenuous "you know". We're back in the world of boyhood adventure, where bouncing barrels down the stairs of empty houses is mischievous fun because they smash and make a glorious noise.

But beyond these obvious strengths it is Huck's regional accent that makes this passage, and indeed the rest of the novel, so aurally memorable. He writes with a noticable drawl. Twain was of course perfectly aware of it, delighting in his discovery that the language of his boyhood, its rich, colloquial looseness, might be turned into literary art. (As a public speaker in later years he was said to exaggerate his own speech pattern for the same reason.) And more: he was explicitly proud of the fact that, in his judgment, he had captured the authentic note of the American provinces. In a short preface he tells the reader to expect at least six shades "of the backwoods South-Western dialect," adding: "The shadings have not been done in any hap-hazard fashion, or by guess-work; but painstakingly, and with the trustworthy guidance and support of personal familiarity with these several forms of speech."

Michael Egan, *Mark Twain's* Huckleberry Finn: *Race, Class and Society.* London: Sussex University Press, 1977, pp. 69–71.

The Boy and the River

Huckleberry Finn is a great book because it is about a god—about, that is, a power which seems to have a mind and will of its own, and which to men of moral imagination appears to embody a great moral idea.

Huck himself is the servant of the river-god, and he comes very close to being aware of the divine nature of the being he serves. The world he inhabits is perfectly equipped to accommodate a deity, for it is full of presences and meanings which it conveys by natural signs and also by preternatural omens and taboos: to look at the moon over the left shoulder, to shake the tablecloth after sundown, to handle a snakeskin, are ways of offending the obscure and prevalent spirits. Huck is at odds, on moral and aesthetic grounds, with the only form of established religion he knows, and his very intense moral life may be said to derive almost wholly from his love of the river. He lives in a perpetual adoration of the Mississippi's power and charm. Huck, of course, always expresses himself better than he can know, but nothing draws upon his gift of speech like his response to his deity. After every sally into the social life of the shore, he returns to the river with relief and thanksgiving; and at each return, regular and explicit as a chorus in a Greek tragedy, there is a hymn of praise to the god's beauty, mystery, and strength, and to his noble grandeur in contrast with the pettiness of men.

Generally the god is benign, a being of long sunny days and spacious nights. But, like any god, he is also dangerous and deceptive. He generates fogs which bewilder, and contrives echoes and false distances which confuse. His sand bars can ground and his hidden snags can mortally wound a great steamboat. He can cut away the solid earth from under a man's feet and take his house with it. The sense of the danger of the river is what saves the book from any touch of the sentimentality and moral ineptitude of most works which contrast the life of nature with the life of society.

The river itself is only divine; it is not ethical and good. But its nature seems to foster the goodness of those who love it and try to fit themselves to its ways. And we must observe that we cannot make—that Mark Twain does not make—an absolute opposition between the river and human society. To Huck much of the charm of the river life is human: it is the raft and the wigwam and Jim. He has not run away from Miss Watson and the Widow Douglas and his brutal father to a completely individualistic liberty, for in Jim he finds his true father. . . . The boy and the Negro slave form a family, a primitive community—and it is a community of saints.

> Lionel Trilling, "Introduction," *The Adventures of Huckleberry Finn*. New York: Holt, Rinehart and Winston, 1950. Rpt. in Lionel Trilling, *The Liberal Imagination: Essays in Literature and Society*. New York: Scribner's, 1950.

The King, the Duke, and the Rogue/Con Man Tradition

A tradition almost as old as prose narrative joins to the novel another tributary of world literature when a purely American wandering brings two further creatures of twilight to the raft. The Duke of Bilgewater and the Lost Dauphin were born of Mark's inexhaustible delight in worthlessness, but are many-sided. Pretension of nobility is one of his commonest themes, here wrought into pure comedy. The Duke is akin to characters in the other books; the King embodies a legend widespread and unimaginably glorious on the frontier. The ambiguity surrounding the death of Louis XVII gave to history riots, dynasties and social comedies that still absorb much reverence in Florence and Paris. It gave mythology a superb legend, which at once accommodated itself to American belief. Up the river from New Orleans, one of the most pious repositories of allegiance, stories of the dethroned Bourbon gratified believers during three generations. The legend must have entertained Mark's boyhood but the circumstances of his Dauphin suggest that he more enjoyed the appearance of Eleazar Williams, who became an international celebrity in 1853. The whole course of his life probably gave him no more satisfying exhibition of the race's folly than the discovery of a Bourbon king in the person of this Mohawk half-breed turned Christian and missionary, who had systematically defrauded his church and his people. The story is one of the occasional ecstasies with which history rewards the patient mind.

The two rogues are formed from the nation's scum. They are products of chance and opportunity, drifters down rivers and across the countryside in the service of themselves. The Duke has sold medicines, among them a preparation to remove tartar from the teeth; he has acted tragedy and can sling a lecture sometimes; he can teach singing-geography school or take a turn to mesmerism or phrenology when there's a chance. The King can tell fortunes and can cure cancer or paralysis by the laying on of hands; but preaching, missionarying, and the temperance revival are his best lines. American universals meet here; once more, this is a whole history, and into these drifters is poured an enormous store of the nation's experience. They have begotten hordes of successors since 1885 but none that joins their immortality. They belong with Colonel Sellers: they are the pure stuff of comedy. Their destiny is guile: to collect the tax which freedom and wit levy on respectability. Their voyage is down a river deep in the American continent; they are born of a purely American scene. Yet the river becomes one of the world's roads and these disreputables join, of right, a select fellowship. They are Diana's foresters: the brotherhood that receives them, approving their passage, is immortal in the assenting dreams of literature. Such freed spirits as [Rabelais's]

Panurge, [Shakespeare's] Falstaff, [Alain-René Lesage's] Gil Blas and the [Anatole France's] Abbé Coignard are of that fellowship; no Americans except the Duke and the Dauphin have joined it. None seems likely to.

> Bernard DeVoto, *Mark Twain's America*. Lincoln: University of Nebraska Press, 1997, pp. 318–20.

Twain's Condemnation of Mississippi River Valley Society

The moral center of the novel focuses in the intense relationship between Huck and Jim, but . . . the panoramic sweep of Huck's journey in search of his father also opens to view a whole civilization, and the wrath of Twain's judgment of that civilization is the novel's most Biblical quality. Entering many houses in his quest for truth and love, Huck calls only the raft his home, a fact which symbolizes at the broadest reach of social implication Twain's massive condemnation of the society of the Great Valley as he knew it in the tragic quarter of a century before the Civil War.

When, at the beginning of the novel, Huck is sworn into Tom Sawyer's gang and introduced to Miss Watson's piousness, he is thereby initiated into the two mysteries of the society which offer—respectively—an institutionalized version of truth and love: romanticism and religion. For Tom, life is a circus, a romantic adventure story. Turnips are "julery" and Sunday school picnickers are "Spanish merchants and rich A-rabs," and Tom denounces Huck as a "numskull" for his literal-mindedness about these marvels. Huck, however, who understands that the fine spectacle of lights twinkling in a village late at night means that "there was sick folks, maybe," knows that romanticism is a way of faking the nature of reality, and when he temporarily forgets this, when he disregards Jim's warning and boards an abandoned steamboat to have an adventure of which Tom Sawyer would have approved, he comes close to losing his life. (The fact that the steamboat is named the "Walter Scott" is scarcely accidental, for in *Life on the Mississippi* Twain had already blasted the Scott-intoxication of the South as "in great measure responsible" for the Civil War.) But the novel's bitterest attack on the romantic imagination occurs in two interrelated and successive chapters, 21 and 22. In the latter chapter, Huck goes to a circus, sees a drunken man weaving around the ring on a horse, and is terribly distressed, although the crowd roars with delight. But it is not Huck's charming naïveté in not recognizing that the drunkard is a clown that Twain condemns, it is the callousness of the crowd. For this circus scene depends upon the preceding chapter, which really does involve a drunk, the drunken Boggs, who weaves down the street on horseback, shouting insults at Colonel Sherburn. When Sherburn mortally wounds Boggs, a crowd gathers excitedly around the drunkard to watch him die. Everyone is tremendously pleased—except Huck, and the dying man's daughter. Thus by this juxtaposition of episodes, each of which contrasts the boy's sympathetic concern with the gleeful howling of the crowd, does Twain lay bare the depravity of a society that views life as a circus, as some kind of romantic show.

For Miss Watson, life is a moral certainty. Bible readings and daily prayers fill her smug world with assurances. She tells Huck that if he will pray every day he will get whatever he asks for, and when he prays for fish hooks without being able to "make it work," she calls him a fool, just as Tom had called him a numskull. Yet it is Miss Watson, prattling of Providential mercy, who treats Nigger Jim severely, who despite her promise to him that she would never sell him away from his wife and children, can't resist the sight of a stack of money and agrees to sell him down the river. If romanticism is a lie, religion is a monumental lovelessness, a terrible hypocrisy. When Huck goes to church with the Grangerfords, the minister preaches a sermon on brotherly love to a congregation made up of men armed to the teeth and panting to kill one another; when the King pretends he is infused with divine grace in order to con the camp meeting, he is only acting out Miss Watson's hypocrisies on the level of farce. But once again, as in his attack on life as a circus, Twain's most withering blast at lovelessness and hypocrisy is delivered by juxtaposing two chapters with a vengeance.

The last paragraph of Chapter 23 is perhaps the most poignant moment in the entire novel, for it is here that Jim relates to Huck how his daughter, after recovering from scarlet fever, became a mysteriously disobedient child. Even when Jim had slapped her and sent her sprawling she refused to obey his orders, but just as he was going for her again, he realized what was wrong: "De Lord God Amighty fogive po' ole Jim, kaze he never gwyne to fogive hisself as long's he live! Oh, she was plumb deef en dumb, Huck, plumb deef en dumb—en I'd ben a-treat'n her so!" On the last page of Chapter 24, the King and the Duke launch their scheme for robbing the Wilks girls of their inheritance, with the King pretending to be a parson and the Duke acting the part of a deaf mute. When viewed beside Jim's sorrow and compassion for his deaf-and-dumb daughter, the spectacle of the two frauds talking on their hands is sickening—"It was enough," says Huck, "to make a body ashamed of the human race."

Kenneth Lynn, "Huck and Jim," in *Mark Twain: A Profile*, edited by Justin Kaplan. New York: Hill and Wang, 1967, pp. 131–33.

Chronology

1835
Mark Twain born Samuel Langhorne Clemens in Florida, Missouri, on November 30.

1839
The Clemens family moves to Hannibal, Missouri.

1847
John Marshall Clemens, the author's father, dies.

1848
Sam is apprenticed to Joseph Ament, owner of the *Hannibal Courier*.

1850
Orion Clemens, the author's brother, publishes the Hannibal *Western Union*.

1851
Sam works for his brother at the *Western Union*.

1852
Harriet Beecher Stowe publishes *Uncle Tom's Cabin*.

1855
Walt Whitman publishes *Leaves of Grass*.

1857
Sam begins his apprenticeship as a steamboat pilot on the Mississippi.

1858
Sam's younger brother, Henry, dies in a steamboat explosion.

1859
Sam receives his pilot's license.

1860
Lincoln is elected president of the United States.

1861
Confederate forces attack Fort Sumter, South Carolina; Sam briefly serves in the Confederate forces; Sam and Orion travel to Carson City, Nevada.

1862
Sam works for the Virginia City *Territorial Enterprise.*

1863
Lincoln signs the Emancipation Proclamation; Sam first uses the pseudonym "Mark Twain."

1864
Twain moves to San Francisco; Lincoln is elected to a second term.

1865
Robert E. Lee surrenders at Appomattox, Virginia, ending the Civil War; Lincoln is assassinated by John Wilkes Booth, an unemployed actor, on April 14; Twain publishes his first story, "The Celebrated Jumping Frog of Calaveras County," in the *New York Saturday Press*; ratification of the Thirteenth Amendment to the Constitution on December 18 abolishes slavery.

1866
Twain travels to the Sandwich Islands (now Hawaii); after his return, he lectures in San Francisco; he meets Olivia (Livy) Langdon on February 4.

1869
Twain becomes engaged to Livy; he embarks on a lecture tour; *The Innocents Abroad* is published.

1870
Twain and Olivia Langdon are married on February 2; on November 7, Langdon Clemens is born.

1871
Twain moves to Hartford, Connecticut.

1872
Roughing It is published; Olivia Susan "Susy" Clemens is born; Langdon Clemens dies on June 2; Twain sails for England in August.

1873
The Gilded Age is published; family spends summer in England and Europe; Twain lectures in England.

1874
Twain returns to the United States; Clara Langdon Clemens is born.

1876
The Adventures of Tom Sawyer is published.

1878–1879
Twain lives in Germany and Italy.

1880
Jane Lampton "Jean" Clemens is born; *A Tramp Abroad* is published.

1881
The Prince and the Pauper is published.

1883
Life on the Mississippi is published.

1884
The Adventures of Huckleberry Finn is published in Great Britain.

1885
The Adventures of Huckleberry Finn is published in the United States.

1889
A Connecticut Yankee in King Arthur's Court is published.

1890
Twain invests in the Paige typesetting machine.

1893
Frederick Jackson Turner's "Frontier Thesis" declares that the American wilderness no longer exists.

1895
The Tragedy of Pudd'nhead Wilson, Tom Sawyer Abroad, and *Personal Recollections of Joan of Arc* are published; Twain undertakes a world tour.

1896
Susy Clemens dies; *Tom Sawyer, Detective* is published.

1897
Following the Equator is published.

1900
The Man That Corrupted Hadleyburg is published.

1904
Livy Clemens dies.

1909
Jean Clemens dies.

1910
Mark Twain dies on April 21.

1916
The Mysterious Stranger is published.

Works Consulted

Major Editions of Huckleberry Finn

Mark Twain. *The Adventures of Huckleberry Finn*. "Introduction" by Justin Kaplan; "Foreword" and "Addendum" by Victor Doyno. New York: Random House, 1996.

————, *The Adventures of Huckleberry Finn*. Berkeley: University of California Press, 1985.

————, *The Adventures of Huckleberry Finn: A Norton Critical Edition*. Ed. Sculley Bradley, Richmond Croom Beatty, E. Hudson Long, and Thomas Cooley. New York: Norton, 1977.

————, *The Adventures of Huckleberry Finn*. New York: Bantam, 1965.

Also by Mark Twain

Mark Twain, *The Adventures of Tom Sawyer*. Berkeley: University of California Press, 1984. The predecessor to *Huck Finn*; a humorous boy's book about life in a town along the Mississippi River.

————, *The Autobiography of Mark Twain*. New York: Harper & Row, 1959. Humorous account of the author's life notable for its "stretchers."

————, *The Celebrated Jumping Frog of Calaveras County and other Sketches*. New York: Oxford University Press, 1996. Contains Mark Twain's famous first short story in addition to other short works.

————, *A Connecticut Yankee in King Arthur's Court*. Berkeley: University of California Press, 1984. The story of a nineteenth-century factory worker who wakes up one day in the court of King Arthur.

————, "Fenmore Cooper's Literary Offenses," in *Great Short Works of Mark Twain*. Ed. Justin Kaplan. New York: Harper & Row, 1967, p. 170. Twain's notorious attack on Cooper's writing and romanticism.

————, *Following The Equator: A Journey Around the World*. New York: Dover, 1989. This travel book recounts Twain's world lecture tour of 1895–96.

————, *The Guilded Age: A Tale of To-day*. New York: New American Library, 1985. Co-written with Charles Dudley

Warner, this satirical novel lent its name to an entire nineteenth-century period of American history.

———, *Huck Finn and Tom Sawyer Among the Indians and Other Unfinished Stories*. Berkeley: University of California Press, 1989. An unfinished potboiler, this is a sequel to *Huck Finn*.

———, *The Innocents Abroad*. New York: New American Library, 1997. Twain's first travel book pokes fun at both American tourists and the supposed superiority of European culture.

———, *Life on the Mississippi*. New York: Bantam, 1981. Twain's account of his escapades as a steamboat pilot on the Mississippi River.

Mark Twain's Letters. Ed. Albert Bigelow Paine. New York: Harper & Brothers, 1917.

Mark Twain, *The Prince and the Pauper*. Berkeley: University of California Press, 1979. A tale of a switch between look-alikes, the king of England and a poor street urchin.

———, *Roughing It*. Berkeley: University of California Press, 1983. Autobiographical tale of Twain's journey out west with his brother.

———, *A Tramp Abroad*. New York: Penguin Books, 1997. This travel book is based on the Twain family's 1878 trip to Europe.

Biographies of Mark Twain

Everett Emerson, *Mark Twain: A Literary Life*. Philadelphia: University of Pennsylvania Press, 2000. A study of the author that places his work in its biographical context.

Andrew Hoffman, *Inventing Mark Twain: The Lives of Samuel Langhorne Clemens*. New York: William Morrow, 1997. The most recent comprehensive biography of Twain. Hoffman sheds light on the influence of Twain's early life on his writings.

William Dean Howells, *My Mark Twain*. New York: Harper & Brothers, 1910. Fellow novelist Howells recalls his forty-year friendship with Mark Twain.

Justin Kaplan, *Mr. Clemens and Mark Twain: A Biography*. New York: Simon & Schuster, 1966. A highly regarded scholarly biography written by a Pulitzer Prize winner.

John Lauber, *The Making of Mark Twain: A Biography*. New York: American Heritage, 1985. Follows Twain's life from childhood to his marriage to Olivia Langdon.

Robert Keith Miller, *Mark Twain*. New York: Frederick Ungar, 1983. A readable critical biography that links Twain's life to his works.

Albert Bigelow Paine, *Mark Twain: A Biography. The Personal and Literary Life of Samuel Langhorne Clemens*. 3 vols. New York: Harper & Brothers, 1912. The authorized version of the novelist's life written by a man who became a good friend in the course of writing the book.

Luke Pease, "Mark Twain Talks," *Portland Oregonian*, August 11, 1895. A newspaper article in which Twain discusses his writings with a reporter.

Henry Nash Smith and William M. Gibson, eds., *Mark Twain–Howells Letters*. Cambridge: Harvard University Press, 1960. Correspondence between the two noted authors and friends.

Dixon Wechter, *Sam Clemens of Hannibal*. Boston: Houghton Mifflin, 1952. Traces the influence of young Sam Clemens's life in Hannibal, Missouri, on the writings of Mark Twain.

Resa Willis, *Mark and Livy: The Love Story of Mark Twain and the Woman Who Almost Tamed Him*. New York: Atheneum, 1992. Details the relationship between Samuel and his wife Olivia Clemens.

Literary Criticism

John C. Bird, "'These Leather-Face People': Huck and the Moral Act of Lying," *Studies in American Fiction* 15, no. 1, spring 1987, p. 71. A study of the manner in which Huck lies to other characters in the novel.

Walter Blair, *Mark Twain and Huck Finn*. Berkeley: University of California Press, 1960. A detailed study of the making of the novel.

Van Wyck Brooks, *The Ordeal of Mark Twain*. 1920. Rev. ed., New York: Dutton, 1933. Important early study of the novelist's struggle to write; influenced critics for many years to come.

Jocelyn Chadwick-Joshua, *The Jim Dilemma: Reading Race in Huckleberry Finn*. Jackson: University of Mississippi Press, 1998. An African American critic defends the historical importance of the novel.

Katie De Koster, Ed., *Readings on The Adventures of Huckleberry Finn*. San Diego: Greenhaven Press, 1998. A wide range of essays on the novel; includes a biography.

Bernard DeVoto, *Mark Twain's America*. Lincoln: University of Nebraska Press, 1997. This classic response to Van Wyck Brooks's *The Ordeal of Mark Twain* was first published in 1932.

Victor Doyno, *Writing* Huck Finn: *Mark Twain's Creative Process*. Philadelphia: University of Pennsylvania Press, 1993. Analyzes the composition of the novel and presents newly discovered omitted passages.

Clifton Fadiman, *Huckleberry Finn: Three Filmed Lessons in the Humanities*. Encyclopedia Britannica Films, 1965. A noted literary scholar provides an overview of the novel in three parts.

Shelley Fisher Fishkin, *Lighting Out for the Territory: Reflections on Mark Twain and American Culture*. New York: Oxford University Press, 1997. In this collection of essays, Fishkin explores Twain's enduring relevance in American culture.

———, *Was Huck Black? Mark Twain and African-American Voices*. New York: Oxford University Press, 1994. Seeks to demonstrate that Huck's voice in the novel is derived from African American speech.

Richard Lederer, *The Miracle of Language*. New York: Pocket, 1991. A varied collection of essays in appreciation of the English language.

James S. Leonard, Thomas A. Tenney, and Thadious M. Davis, eds., *Satire or Evasion? Black Perspectives on Huckleberry Finn*. Durham, NC: Duke University Press, 1992. Prominent African American critics express their views of the novel and its controversies.

Robert Sattelmeyer and J. Donald Crowley, eds., *One Hundred Years of Huckleberry Finn: The Boy, His Book, and American Culture*. Columbia: University of Missouri Press, 1985. A wide-ranging collection of essays on the novel; includes a bibliography of criticism.

John H. Wallace, "*Huckleberry Finn* Is Racist Trash," *Chicago Sun-Times,* May 25, 1984, p. A23. One of the most scathing contemporary attacks on the novel is based on its alleged racism.

Historical Background

Ira Berlin, Marc Favreau, and Steven F. Miller, eds., *Remembering Slavery: African Americans Talk About Their Personal Experiences of Slavery and Freedom*. New York: New Press,

1998. Interviews with former slaves conducted by the Federal Writers Project in the early 1930s.

John W. Blassingame, *The Slave Community: Plantation Life in the Antebellum South*. Rev. ed. New York: Oxford University Press, 1979. A classic study of the culture of American slavery.

William Dudley, ed., *African Americans: Opposing Viewpoints*. San Diego: Greenhaven Press, 1997. This anthology of essays documents the history of African Americans from the time of slavery to recent controversies over affirmative action.

Henry Louis Gates Jr., ed., *The Classic Slave Narratives*. New York: Penguin, 1987. In these autobiographical narratives, black slaves proclaim their humanity

Vincent Harding, *There Is a River: The Black Struggle for Freedom in America*. Rev. ed. New York: Harcourt Brace Jovanovich, 1991. A study of African American slavery up until the Civil War.

Nathan Irvin Huggins, *Black Odyssey: The African-American Ordeal in Slavery*. New York: Vintage Books, 1990. Traces African American history from slavery to emancipation.

Edwin McDowell, "From Twain, a Letter on Debt to Blacks," *New York Times*, March 14, 1895, sec I, p. 1. A letter from Twain offers to pay the tuition of one of the first black students to attend Yale Law School and suggests Twain's opposition to racism.

Index

Picture Credits

About the Author

Gary Wiener has taught high school English for fifteen years and has also served as an English department coordinator for ten years. He earned a Ph.D. in English and American literature from the University of Rochester in 1986. He is the editor of several books for Greenhaven Press, including *Readings on Walt Whitman* and *Readings on Gulliver's Travels*. He is currently assistant principal at Greece Olympia High School in Rochester, New York. He lives in Pittsford, New York, with his wife, Iris; his son, Michael; and his daughter, Mollie.